REBUILDING

The Church's hold on

Stephen Platten

First published in Great Britain in 2007

Society for Promoting Christian Knowledge
36 Causton Street
London SW1P 4ST

The publisher and author acknowledge with thanks permission to reproduce extracts
from the following:
Sidney Keyes, 'War Poet', in *Collected Poems*, Carcenet, 2002;
Louise MacNeice, 'Snow', in *Collected Poems*, Faber & Faber, 1966;
Herbert Read, 'To a Conscript of 1940', in Hugh Haughton (ed.), *Second World War
Poems*, Faber & Faber, 2004;
R. S. Thomas, 'The Kingdom', *Later Poems*, Macmillan, 1983. Copyright © Kunjana
Thomas.

Every effort has been made to acknowledge fully the sources of material reproduced
in this book. The publisher apologizes for any omissions that may remain and, if
notified, will ensure that full acknowledgements are made in a subsequent edition.

British Library Cataloguing-in-Publication Data
A catalogue record for this book is available from the British Library

ISBN 978–0–281–05697–2

1 3 5 7 9 10 8 6 4 2

Typeset by Graphicraft Limited, Hong Kong
Printed in Great Britain by Ashford Colour Press

Produced on paper from sustainable forests

Contents

About the author

Stephen Platten is Bishop of Wakefield. He taught theology at Lincoln Theological College. Later he was the Archbishop of Canterbury's Secretary for Ecumenical Affairs before becoming Dean of Norwich in 1995. Stephen is the author of *Pilgrims* and *Augustine's Legacy*, and is the author and editor of several other books, including, with Christopher Lewis, *Dreaming Spires?*: *Cathedrals in a new age*, published by SPCK (2006). In 2005 he was appointed Chairman of the Liturgical Commission.

Preface

Work on a book like this involves not simply the author but a host of others who have helped make it possible. I would like to pay particular tribute to Patricia Robertshaw who has typed tirelessly and who has also helped a great deal in the ordering of notes and other editorial detail. Stephen Spencer has kindly read through the entire text, sometimes more than once and helped me to avoid some of my worst potential pitfalls. I am also grateful to both Marlene Beresford and Jane Butterfield for their support in some of the final typing and editing. Joanna Moriarty has been a most understanding and positive editor. As ever any final mistakes which survive must be put down to me alone.

To Rosslie, Aidan and Esther, Gregory and Gillian and most especially to the next generation, in the person of Alice.

Introduction

And did those feet in ancient time
Walk upon England's mountains green?
And was the holy Lamb of God
On England's pleasant pastures seen?
And did the countenance divine
Shine forth upon our clouded hills?
And was Jerusalem builded here
Among those dark satanic mills?

Bring me my bow of burning gold!
Bring me my arrows of desire!
Bring me my spear! O clouds, unfold!
Bring me my chariot of fire!
I will not cease from mental fight,
Nor shall my sword sleep in my hand,
Till we have built Jerusalem
In England's green and pleasant land.

William Blake 1757–1827

Living in West Yorkshire, it is not difficult to appreciate the images which Blake used in his powerful poem. Still the 'clouded hills' and 'satanic mills' stand ironically, both in juxtaposition and in continuity with each other. For the West Yorkshire landscape is robust and the buildings equally so. Alongside Lancashire, the Black Country, Derbyshire and the north east of England, this part of Yorkshire was one of the classical growth points of the industrial revolution. Religion and the new industry did not easily walk hand in hand. Dissent responded more sensitively and more effectively than did the established Church. Methodist and independent chapels still stand almost as the religious equivalents to the mills that surround them. They are often built in a similarly robust and even triumphant architecture. Sadly, like the mills which are their 'cousins', they now most often stand silent.

It is ironic too that Blake's 'Jerusalem' should have taken on the form of almost an alternative English national anthem. For

Blake was no conventional patriot. Politically he was a radical, supporting the American and French revolutions; he was a friend of Tom Paine. The terrible outcome of the French Revolution, however, transformed the nature of Blake's rebelliousness and led him away from the political undertones of his earlier poetry towards a later Christian mood. But Blake never became the pious hermit as he is described by some. He was no conventional Christian and was a trenchant critic of the established Church of England. His Christian writings were as radical and rebellious as were his political poems. His Christianity was heterodox, placing the Son and Father as almost polar opposites; Christ was the holder of divine goodness and the Father was a tyrannous despot. This partly mirrored Blake's own difficulties with human authority. Still, there is no doubting Blake's prophetic character, even if we disagree with his conclusions.

Blake's famous poem stands at the beginning of this book not because the argument which follows resonates with that of Blake's political or religious ideas. They still challenge but they belong to their own time. No, Blake's poem is here because in his own way he raised the issue, in a most radical manner, which has prompted this book. The book is about whether the Church in England, lost the hearts of the people of England. If it did so, did it happen more than once? If the answer to both these questions lies in the affirmative then what lessons can we learn from an analysis of this?

There is a rhetorical feel to those opening lines of the first stanza of 'Jerusalem'. Surely Jerusalem *was* builded here? At the same time, however, there is a powerful sense of what has been lost. The second verse brings all of Blake's radical passion to bear on the issue: 'Bring me my chariot of fire!' There is no doubt that Blake believed that Jerusalem was to be rebuilt, but did that really ever happen? If it did not happen could it happen now? Only, perhaps, if we begin to understand those occasions when Jerusalem was destroyed, some of which may have occurred long after Blake completed his visionary poem.

Stephen Platten
Epiphany 2007

1

For Georgia, England and St George?

In May 1993, George Carey, then Archbishop of Canterbury, paid an official visit to Patriarch Ilya II of Georgia, the Catholicos – Patriarch of All Georgia. It was a momentous visit for more than one reason. To begin with, it was the first ever official visit of an Archbishop of Canterbury to the Georgian Orthodox Church. It was part of a wider journey, which embraced also the Patriarch of All the Russias, in Moscow, and the Catholicos of the Armenian Apostolic Orthodox Church, in the holy monastery at Etchmiadzin. But it was a unique visit for a very different reason too. This was the first high-level visit from the Church of England since the collapse of the Soviet Union. What would it reveal about the state of religion in Georgia?

At least a partial answer could be gleaned from the Archbishop's attendance at the liturgy for the feast of St George, in St George's Church on Rustaveili Avenue, right at the heart of Tbilisi. (The Georgian Orthodox celebrate St George on 6 May and in November, but not on 23 April as in the western calendar.) The liturgy reflected all that one might expect of Chalcedonian Orthodoxy – colour, drama and, in this case, the additional unique beauty of Georgian liturgical music. But the Archbishop's party was most moved by the thronging numbers of worshippers present, and their self-evident piety. Throughout the four-hour liturgy the church was packed, and people came and went as the morning wore on. The congregation included an extraordinary cross-section of Georgian society: young children and babes in arms; teenagers and men in their early twenties; middle-aged couples and pious elderly men and women. It was a powerful spectacle. Seventy years of enforced atheism in the country which had bred Josef Stalin, one of the most brutal dictators of the twentieth century, had failed to stifle the religious impulses of the population. Stalin, a former seminarian, had reserved his most tyrannical

1

repression of Church and society at large for the people of his native Georgia. Yet despite all this, the ancient faith lives on.

This experience provoked sharp and emotional responses within all of us who were members of the Archbishop's party. Perhaps the most notable reaction, from one member of our group, went something like this. 'All these people, on entering the church, knew exactly what to do, how to worship, when to sing or chant. Religion is still natural to them. Christianity flows through their bloodstreams; it is there pulsing through their hearts. Isn't it sobering? I wonder when precisely the Church in England lost the hearts of the English people?' Each of us pondered this and acknowledged the perceptiveness of the reflection. For rarely, if ever, would one encounter such spontaneous and immediate religiosity in the mainstream English churches. Even taking account of the variations between cultures, and the difference in expression of religious instincts in different ethnic groups, there seemed to be a lesson to be learnt. St George's, Rustaveili Avenue, on that feast day, manifested most powerfully an innate and natural religiosity, which, at least on an initial reflection, appears to be part of the human condition.

Affirming the existence of such objective natural impulses and perceptions is not a fashionable belief to hold at present. This is not only true in religion, but in other realms of human experience too. So, the suggestion that there is a 'natural law' running through creation, open to discernment within the human mind, is rejected, for example, by many moralists. Similarly, the suggestion that one might construct a 'natural theology', beginning with the nature of the universe and deducing from that the existence of a transcendent being, that is a God, has also been exposed to a radical critique – Karl Barth, the most incisive critic of natural theology, still seems to have as many followers as ever. Nonetheless, despite these serious intellectual attacks on naturalistic philosophies and theologies, these instincts still persist. Moral philosophers and students of jurisprudence continue to argue for at least a 'natural morality'; morals of a general nature can be deduced from that pattern of behaviour that contributes to human flourishing and fulfilment. Some moral philosophers, and many theologians, still argue then for a form of natural law.[1] Furthermore, poets, writers and a significant number of Christian theologians still opine that theology should both take account of revelation through Holy Scripture and equally reflect upon the nature of creation, and of what that may tell us of God. Creation may, of course, alternately appear opaque or transparent to God and providence but, still, natural theology is a respectable and religiously valuable activity. Wordsworth characterized this well in his 'Ode – Intimations of Immortality from Recollections of Early Childhood':

> There was a time when meadow, grove, and stream.
> The earth, and every common sight,
> To me did seem
> Apparelled in celestial light,
> The glory and the freshness of a dream
> It is not now as it hath been of yore;

Yet still, despite the passing years, at the very end of the poem he can reflect:

> To me the merest flower that blows can give
> Thoughts that do often lie too deep for tears.[2]

Such reflections, then, on natural morality and natural theology return us to our starting point: that is, to our deepest natural human instincts in the realms of religious faith. Is there such a thing as 'natural religion'? What really was going on, on that morning in Tbilisi in May 1993? Is religious faith something that is natural, and if so are there ways of nurturing it or producing positive human reactions to it? Is it true that the Church in England did resonate with the natural religiosity of the hearts of the people of England, perhaps earlier in the Middle Ages, and at some point(s) ceased to do so? If that is the case, then when precisely did it happen, and can those hearts be won again for Christ, to put it in Christian missionary language? This is not to suggest, of course, that natural religiosity and the Christian faith are the same thing.

*

In attempting to answer this intriguing and most important question, we shall find ourselves straddling the borderlands between theology, literature, anthropology, sociology and perhaps even social psychology. Furthermore, much of our analysis will also carry us over into the realm of historical study. How

3

does it look at different points in human history? If one asks these sorts of questions of anthropologists, sociologists and other human scientists, their first plea would be to look for a controlled example. In other words, the aim would be to isolate a group of people and then apply different conditions to that sample and monitor the effects. Do they have natural religious instincts, and if so how are they nurtured? There are two reasons why it is particularly difficult to produce a controlled example in this case. First of all, how could one conceivably isolate a group religiously in this way? The nature of society is such that influences bear continuously on groups, both diachronically and synchronically – that is, across history and within cultures geographically at the same time. Second, it is impossible to imagine applying such influences artificially – how would one persuade either the control sample or the different purveyors of the Christian faith to engage in such an activity?

There is, however, one fascinating example which existed for some centuries just on the edge of modern western civilization. This takes us into the eastern reaches of the Atlantic Ocean. The islands of St Kilda exist on the edge of our world. Almost 50 miles west of the Outer Hebrides, these jagged islands and rocky stacks are so isolated as to generate their own weather patterns; this has helped them to become still more remote, simply by making it difficult for others to reach them. Even with modern maritime methods, there are many occasions when ships cannot approach the islands, let alone drop their anchors in the harbour at Village Bay, the only safe anchorage in the archipelago. The islands are often described as 'a world apart', and they do offer the religious commentator and sociologist of religion a unique controlled sample, albeit with a fairly limited critical history in regard to documentary evidence. The landscape of the islands is itself remarkable. At Conachair the cliffs rise to a height of 1,400 feet, higher than at any other place in the British Isles. Alongside Hirta, the main island, are smaller islets and jagged stacks sticking up out of the Atlantic Ocean. Stac Lee and Stac an Armin are bare rocks rearing up from an often tempestuous sea.

As well as being a World Heritage Site, St Kilda is the largest bird sanctuary in Britain, with more than one and a half million birds, and the largest gannetry in the world, with over 400,000 pairs of gannets. The islands are not friendly to human habitation.

The annual rainfall is upwards of 50 inches, and for eight months of the year the archipelago is subjected to powerful storms and terrifyingly high winds. Approaching the islands is in itself an awe-inspiring experience, with cloud frequently hanging in mid-sky so that the highest cliffs and the needle-pointed stacks surface above the clouds, leaving behind the bases of the islands below, which are thus seen underneath the clouds.

The origins of the people of St Kilda are lost in the mists of history; they were probably Celtic in their antecedents. In the seventh and eighth centuries Scotland was invaded by Norsemen.[3] We have no way of telling whether they settled on St Kilda. Certainly, a number of the names are Norse in origin, but these are largely landmarks which may have been named by seafarers from the sea – although for the names to have stuck it seems likely that some Norse may have landed on the islands in those early centuries. Earthenware cooking pots similar to those used by Vikings have been discovered on Hirta. Clearly, the Celtic, or possibly Celtic–Norse, inhabitants would in earliest times have espoused some sort of paganism. But to leap to religion at this point is premature.

The situation of St Kilda meant that both the means of subsistence and the social structures were unique to this isolated civilization. The vast number of gannets has already been adverted to; they formed part of the St Kildan's staple diet. But it was another seabird which proved to be more useful still in feeding the population. This was the fulmar petrel. The fulmar secretes a vile-smelling oil in its stomach which it can spit over a distance of some two or three feet. The fulmar petrel, then, not only provided meat but also, through fulmar oil, fuel for lamps and heating, and down for beds, also an important export crop, sent via the factor (who effectively managed the estate) to the mainland. From their youth, St Kildan men were trained to scale the cliffs and stacks in pursuit of gannets and fulmars. The fulmars they would strangle so as to keep the precious oil within the dead birds. The birds were also salted down for winter, and so they provided food for all seasons, as well as rent with which to pay the factor. The harvesting of seabirds was hard and dangerous work, but it lay at the heart of the survival and prospering of the community. The male ankles of St Kildans had developed and evolved uniquely to give them the resilience, strength and stamina required for this exhausting work. Evolution had effectively contributed its own part in the survival of this unique human community.

Alongside the harvesting of seabirds went fishing and rudimentary agriculture. There was also a unique breed of sheep, particularly flourishing on the island of Soay. All this meant, of course, that the St Kildans both lived and breathed a dependence upon the harsh natural environment in which they had been placed; nature and the elements meant both life and death to them. The isolated and minute nature of the community (their numbers never exceeded 200) meant too that the political (so to speak) structure of the island was also unique. The entire community took responsibility for the feeding, clothing and housing of all who lived there. They also sought to provide sufficient exports to pay the proprietor – through his factor – the rent. This resulted in what was virtually communitarian socialism. Early each day all the adult men met to discuss what work was to be done. Later this became known by tourists as the St Kilda Parliament. The fact of their isolation, and their small numbers, combined with the vulnerability of life on the archipelago, meant that the St Kildans saw themselves as a community and not as individuals. Distribution would be settled by lot if there were difficulties. There was effectively no hierarchy among the islanders. Those who were sick or vulnerable, through youth or old age, were always given care. The description of the early Christian community in Acts 4.32 described the St Kildan situation well: '. . . no one said that any of the things that he possessed was his own, but they had everything in common.'

This arrangement, however, arose neither through scriptural diktat nor through a romantic socialism. It was the 'natural' product of living in such a challenging and contained environment. But what about religion?

It is often assumed that the name St Kilda implies the apostolate of an early and intrepid missionary, washed up in a boat, following the Celtic pattern of pilgrimage for Christ. The Celtic–Irish Christian view of pilgrimage was indeed one of abandoning yourself to God's grace, casting off in a coracle from the safety of your homeland, and allowing yourself to be 'shipwrecked' wherever the Lord took you. This is the pattern pictured in the semi-legendary voyages of St Brendan.[4] More historically than these legends, it was the impetus that took

Columba to Iona from Derry,[5] and Fursey to Burgh Castle in East Anglia from Lough Corrib near Galway.[6] But the origins of the name St Kilda are entirely without Christian, or, as far as we know, religious association. Indeed, the name St Kilda was probably rarely used by the islanders of their home. The largest island is called Hirta, and the name St Kilda may have come from the way in which the inhabitants pronounced this word. Others say that the name Hirta derives from the old Irish word *hiort*, meaning 'death' or 'gloom', implying that the land of spirits lay beyond the sea. Certainly there is no evidence, nor any reason to believe, that a saint called Kilda ever lived.

Nevertheless, the St Kildans were an intensely religious people. We have already seen why this might be the case. A combination of the sheer grandeur and stupendous nature of their homeland, combined with their dependence on nature and the elements, was likely to make them, at the very least, superstitious, and, more positively, religious. Despite the possible pagan incursions of Norsemen and the equally pagan background of the earlier Celtic tribes, it is likely that the history of Christianity in the archipelago goes back even beyond that of the Scottish mainland. The journeys of monks from the skelligs on the west coast of Ireland have already made their appearances in references to Fursey and his East Anglian voyage.[7] But Fursey is only the tip of the iceberg. For Ireland was a powerhouse of religious fervour and missionary zeal in the sixth century. Pilgrims for Christ set off to arrive in Ireland, Scotland, England and possibly even Scandinavia. St Kilda would have been within the network of routes of these intrepid Christian explorers. Between these early missionary conversions and modern history, however, there is a yawning documentary gap. We have little, if no, knowledge of how precisely that early catholic Christianity transmuted into the radical Presbyterianism born of the Scottish Reformation.

Ignorance as to the precise origins, or not, this drastic transformation did take place, and gave the basic character to St Kildan religion which survived, in various transmuted forms, until the tragic collapse of the island civilization and subsequent evacuation in 1930. Martin Martin, visiting the island in 1697, discovered a people 'governed by the dictates of reason and Christianity'. Other reports suggest that St Kildan Christianity still embraced a joy, born of its Celtic roots. At this time there was no religious minister living on Hirta. Instead, a minister would go out from the Western Isles. That the transfer from catholic religion to Presbyterianism had not been complete this early on is made plain through the journal of Alexander Buchan, who went out as a missionary in 1705. He reflected his purpose as being 'to root out the pagan and Papist superstitious customs so much yet in use amongst the people'. Rarely, however, did ministers remain permanently on the island – for understandable reasons! The later history of the island might make the cynic remark that the continued absence of resident ministers would have offered the best of all possible worlds for St Kildans: sufficient religion to give structure, meaning and godliness to their lives; insufficient religion to repress their natural impulses and even endanger their way of life.

The arrival of John Macdonald in 1822 wrought significant changes. Even he was not a permanent resident, but he did make long stays and left a marked influence. It would be unfair to suggest that he was unpopular in Hirta; people were tearful at his last farewell. He had instituted a well-organized, harsh and puritan Christianity, and this left its negative impression too upon the island community. The natural joy and impulsive love of dance and song was repressed. Also, the natural rhythms of their life, governed by their need to survive and by the extremes of a climate which was unique to the islands, were exchanged for an imposed regime of rigorous religious observance. Macdonald's instincts were not deliberately oppressive, but the effects of his good instincts would leave marks that might ultimately contribute to the death of this tiny remote civilization.

Neil Mackenzie was the first resident minister on St Kilda. He arrived in 1829. In his time the first manse and stone churches were built. He contributed much to the raising of the living standards of the islanders and encouraged them to a new cleanliness and hygiene, as well as helping them better organize the island's agriculture. But, ultimately, it was John Mackay's arrival on St Kilda in 1866 that was to have the most radical effect of all upon the St Kildans. Arguably, Mackay may have been one of the chief architects of the islands' downfall, alongside other factors relating to disease brought from outside, and the undermining effects of a mainland civilization which treated St Kilda as a society of primitive people, almost to be visited as museum pieces or as part of a human zoo. John Mackay instituted a new orthodoxy which went well beyond anything as yet seen on St Kilda. There were three services on each Sunday, keeping the inhabitants in church for six and a half hours or more. From the evening of Saturday till the dawning of the Sabbath no conversation was allowed – only the reading of the Bible out loud was acceptable. The usual austerity of extreme Calvinist Presbyterianism went with this – no musical instrument was allowed in the church. The abolition of such 'idolatry' drove out the final elements of joy in the St Kildan's Christianity. Reading matter was censored, and religion on the islands became little more than rooted in the profoundly caricatured received opinions of that one minister.

It was not just the change in religious practice that was to leave its mark. The social effects of this radicalized religion were more serious still. The patterns of life described, and alluded to earlier on, indicate a rhythm rooted in nature and in the need to harvest food to survive. These new rigorous patterns of church-going interfered with this way of life and destroyed the earlier natural rhythms. The new patterns so dominated life that even when the St Kildans went to adjacent islands to slaughter birds, or to care for their sheep, elders would accompany them. On the remoter islands, too, the islanders would interrupt the natural rhythm with morning and evening prayers. This new religious regime had one further negative effect upon the natural patterns established among the islanders for centuries. Both the minis-ter's own authority and the appointment of elders produced a hierarchy unknown before in the island community. The nat-ural communitarianism began to decline.

To argue that the ultimate demise of the St Kildan community was a direct result of these religious transformations would be an egregious argument, and unsupportable. Nevertheless, this factor was at the least a notable catalyst, and most likely one of three or four key causes in the final collapse of the islanders' civiliza-tion. Much more could be written of St Kildan religion, but these snapshots are brief insights into a developing and changing re-sponse to the natural religiosity of the islanders. In some senses the inherited ways would never die until the final evacuation of the islands. The reality of their belief never faded, and there was an impulse within them to accept the authority of the minister, whoever he turned out to be, and whatever idiosyncrasies he brought with him. After the evacuation in 1930, however, on arrival on the mainland, the islanders would soon sit loose to the religious responses which had helped form their lives. One commentator reflects: 'When the islanders left behind their Bibles in the Church at the evacuation, all but the elderly turned their backs on a form of religion that had so blatantly restricted their happiness.'[8]

Throughout the rest of this book we shall be looking specifically at the experience of the Church *in* England. We shall be attempting to see if there were moments when, because of changes in the ways in which the Church/churches acted (or through the intrusion of the contingencies of history) somehow the ability to respond to humankind's natural religiosity was blunted. The unique experience of St Kilda is helpful in this. Nowhere else in Britain or Ireland did a community live its religious life in complete isolation. Sociological, ecclesiological and even physical changes, then, can be observed at the same time as seeing how a religious response became transmuted. This may make our religious antennae better attuned to noting shifts in England or beyond. These reflections on St Kilda are not presented as a 'knockdown' argument on religiosity and the contingencies of the Church and the world. They are, however, offered as a photographic negative of how things changed in one isolated community. Among the variables that operated there, which of these had parallels in the wider, more open, and diverse world of England? Have they affected responses to natural religiosity in the manner which seems to have happened on St Kilda?

For, ultimately, these experiences were by no means unique to St Kilda. To pick up a similar resonance, again from Scotland, the poet and writer Edwin Muir would forsake the Calvinism of his Orcadian youth with considerable anger. Christianity in his youth had been a negative force. He expresses this vehemently in lines from his poem 'The Incarnate One':

> The word made flesh is here made word again,
> A word made word in flourish and arrogant crook,
> See there King Calvin with his iron pen,
> And God three angry letters in a book . . .'[9]

Only many years later would Muir return to faith, this time with a more symbolic and sacramental base.

None of this analysis is intended to attack Calvinist Christianity. St Kilda is simply taken as a unique controlled example. Similar things could doubtless be said about other specific forms of Catholic, Orthodox, Anglican or, indeed, Lutheran Christianity. The moral of this particular tale appears to be about how a specific form of religion responds to humanity's natural religiosity. Reflection upon this has implications for individual and social psychology, sociology and, indeed, for the fundamentals of theology itself. How is God made known to us, and how important is it for religion to take note of natural rhythms in society? How do religion and faith relate to those factors which bind human beings together in community? This introduction may help us to explain this in more detail later in this book. Before we conclude this introductory chapter, let us broaden the insights learnt from the religious history of St Kilda. Let us do so particularly in reflecting upon the sharp contrast between present religious observance, first in Britain and Western Europe, and then in the very different religious scene in the USA.

*

We began with a cameo of religious life in post-Soviet Tbilisi, which indicated how faith and religious observance survived even the most brutal of tyrannies. This suggests, as indeed does the vivid tale of life on St Kilda, that religiosity and the religious impulse is a natural instinct. In a recent analysis of faith across the contemporary world, Grace Davie quotes the so-called 'rational choice theory' (RCT).[10] RCT in North America seeks to explain the phenomenon which we style religion. RCT attempts to do what 'secularization theory' has been used for in Europe: that is, it seeks to understand how religion has developed in the modern world, using the USA as a worked example or a case in point. At the heart of RCT stands the premise that the actual demand for religion in human societies remains constant. Davie summarizes the essence of the theory thus: 'Being religious is part of the human condition, given the inability of individuals in themselves to meet many of their deepest needs (not least the security of knowing what happens to them after death).'[11] This statement is not intended to be purely reductionist, explaining religion away through either psychological or sociological needs.

11

Instead, it is both descriptive and phenomenological: it explains the functional significance of religion for humanity, but it is also implicitly theological and philosophical in its argument: it hints at how epistemology – that is, our ability to know God – relates to the practicalities of the human condition.

It is within such categories that Davie analyses the contrasts between American and Western European patterns of religious observance. How is it that the figures for regular churchgoing in the USA remain consistently high when compared with statistics for Britain and Western Europe? The most recent surveys suggest that an average of over 40 per cent of the American population attend weekly, and an even higher proportion monthly. Davie's analysis focuses on two particular significant factors which obtain, and which make the American and European experiences so widely divergent. The first factor stands at the heart of American self-consciousness. It relates to the voluntarist principle, which is there not only in American religion but also more widely within American life. There is an independence from the state, which contrasts with the European historical development of religion; as throughout American life there is an emphasis on freedom of choice, so there is effectively a supermarket of religions in the USA. This, placed alongside that which binds Americans together, gives religion a key function within society. Phrases like 'In God we trust' and 'One nation, one God' lie at the heart. All this, Davie argues, directly relates to the Judaeo-Christian tradition, and so spills out even beyond Christianity alone. An increasingly diverse immigration of people from other faiths may complicate the American scene. Nonetheless, it will not necessarily undermine this religious functionalism. It could, indeed, reinforce it. Religion helps Americans focus their identity as individuals, as communities and as a nation.

For the point at issue is: what binds Americans together in all their diversity and what part does religion – and most notably the Christian faith – play in this? This brings us to the second key factor identified by Grace Davie, which also contrasts the American and European situation. This is the fact that religion cuts vertically into American society, whereas in Europe the cut is horizontal. In other words, religious practice embraces people in every aspect and level of society within the USA; in Europe religion has become associated with power, and sometimes with divisions between social classes. This again relates to religion having been linked with the state in Europe. Hence, as various European peoples have rejected some of the political subjections of the past, so sometimes, if not always, they have rejected elements of the religious connections that were associated with those earlier political institutions and traditions.

This series of reflections brings us full circle to issues about the natural status of religion and its function. In Soviet countries, at least to some degree, the Christian faith's association with key factors within human existence have meant that those natural religious impulses, within both individuals and communities, have survived the exigencies of a tyrannical and atheistic regime. Indeed, in the face of some of the harshnesses and brutalities associated with both Stalin and his successors, religion was one of the few recourses left to people to help make sense of what otherwise could seem to be a meaningless world. It would be romantic and superficial to assume that this has been a universal response within former Soviet republics, where the underlying culture was historically Christian. With some, the overlain years of atheistic communism have taken their toll of religious faith. Even when the credibility of totalitarian socialism failed, faith has remained obscured or rejected by significant numbers within former Soviet states. Furthermore, the association of the Christian faith with the state, alluded to in the case of Western Europe, has manifested itself even more obviously in the Byzantine models of the east. Religion and government were closely intertwined in the Byzantine Empire, and part of the legacy of this was an unhealthy collusion between the ecclesiastical hierarchy and the state in Soviet times. This has left its scars with regard to the credibility of Christian faith following such collusion with tyranny. Nevertheless, despite these caveats, a functional pattern of religious response has emerged – natural to the human condition and well attuned to the rhythm of people's lives.

Similarly, the analysis of life on St Kilda points to some of these contrasts. The very remoteness and harshness of life focused a sharp dependence upon the natural order. Climate, terrain and limited natural resources stimulated an acute religious responsiveness. This was rooted in the natural rhythm of life on the islands, and helped fuel the cultural and celebratory impulses of a community that rejoiced in God, despite the toughness of the context in which they were placed. They too were bound together in a community which had no need of horizontal stratification or division. The arrival of later missionaries, bringing with them both the theological structures and the ecclesiastical hierarchy of an alien world, meant less engagement with natural rhythms and a diminishing sense of one equitable community. This produced an alien culture characterized clearly by Edwin Muir's image of the 'word made word again'. St Kilda's orally transmitted traditions, together with the performative needs of their natural life, were overlain with a very different pattern. After evacuation, this took its toll on the St Kildans' religious responses. The hearts of the people had largely been lost to the Church, and thereby also to the gospel.

Grace Davie's contrast of European and American patterns is illuminating, and is an issue to which we must needs return in the analysis which will follow. How precisely have these responses been affected by changes in English society over the centuries, and can the Christian churches learn from these experiences as they seek to offer the gospel to a new and rapidly changing generation? How can lessons be learnt from the American phenomenon of religion, and have both European and American cultures and societies something to reflect upon in relation to these contrasting patterns?

It would be more than simplistic to talk of there being examples of no religion, bad religion and good religion. Nonetheless, what is beginning to emerge is a sense of religion responding to the natural rhythms encountered within the human condition. Sometimes these may be the 'elemental forces of the universe', to make use of a Pauline phrase. Such forces were at work in St Kilda with the harshness of climate and landscape. In a different way they have come into play in our contemporary society, with a natural response to tragedies and disasters: the death of Princess Diana, the attacks upon the twin towers in New York, the atrocities on the London underground, and numerous natural disasters and human conflicts have begun to elicit very vivid responses from communities and individuals. What does this say about the 'natural roots' of religion and belief in a transcendent deity? Certainly, it suggests that there is some form of elemental religious instinct and God-given response which helps to give meaning where meaning might otherwise be hard to find. In looking at this from the viewpoint of Christian theology, we are coming close to concepts which form the background to a doctrine of *grace*; that is, humanity cannot simply reach out for God through its own efforts – this was the mistake of Pelagius.

Elsewhere, as we have argued, religious responses relate to the nature of human society itself, and how humanity is bound together. The forces of individualism have gathered pace in the past two or three generations, but there remains a key element within the human condition which registers the need to 'belong'. This is closely related to the forces which keep a society functional. For common values are part of what give a community a sense of a binding core of customs and traditions. Grace Davie notes at one point:

> Europe is in the process of removing the 'keystone' in the arch of its value-system without being altogether clear about what should be put in its place. This is clear in the confusion over the status of marriage and other forms of partnership within contemporary European societies.[12]

This book is not primarily about religion and values, but the underlying issues about what bind our society together cannot be dissociated from the healthiness of faith and its ability to respond to the natural foundations of religion. Revelation is an essential part of the Christian faith, but it cannot effectively engage with human beings individually, or in a community, if the natural and rhythmic religious impulses given to human beings through God's grace are ignored.

How can we learn from the history of religious development of the Christian Church in England, and what might this say sociologically, anthropologically and theologically in contrast to the very different scene in the USA?

2

Dismantling the scaffolding

On one occasion there happened to be a great fire in Bishops Lynn, which burned down the Guildhall of the Trinity. This same terrible and serious fire was very likely to have burned down the parish church – dedicated in honour of St Margaret, a stately place and richly honoured – and also the whole town as well, had there been no grace or miracle . . . her confessor, parish priest of St Margaret's Church, took the precious sacrament and went before the fire as devoutly as he could and afterwards brought it back into church again – and the sparks of the fire flew about the church . . . Soon after, three worthy men came into her with snow on their clothes, saying to her, 'Look, Margery, God has shown us great grace and sent us a fair snowstorm to quench the fire with. Be now of good cheer and thank God for it.'[1]

Margery Kempe's *Book* from which those words are taken is a remarkable window into both the mediaeval piety and the life of a significant town in the Middle Ages. The Guild of the Holy Trinity which met in the fire-stricken Guildhall was a rich and most powerful guild. Its rebuilt and great Guildhall survives and is still used as a town hall for this ancient borough. Out of its considerable wealth the guild was generous to deserving causes, including lepers, the lame, the blind and the poor. It had its own chapel in St Margaret's Church and prayers were daily offered for the departed members of the guild; it was effectively a chantry chapel. The chantries were lavishly supported by the great and the good of Bishop's Lynn who were also the pillars who upheld the guild. Countless chantry chapels have survived throughout England, even though their original purpose has been lost. Often they are built into the fabric of the great mediaeval cathedrals or town churches. Sometimes they are separate buildings; in Rotherham and Wakefield, in Yorkshire, there are chapels 'guarding' the bridges leading into the towns.

The existence of such chapels and the pattern of life described in Margery's extraordinary book are powerful indicators of the integrated fabric of life in mediaeval England. It was often difficult to distinguish sacred from secular. Margery, perhaps best described as a minor mystic, travelled widely; she was a surprisingly cosmopolitan figure. She made pilgrimages to Assisi, Rome, Jerusalem and Compostela. She travelled to the English shrines at nearby Walsingham and also to Hailes in Gloucestershire, where she travelled to be renewed by the 'Holy Blood'. Pilgrimage, like chantry chapels, was part of the fabric of life in the Middle Ages and was integrally related to the system of indulgences. Where indulgences were granted, the pilgrim could be assured remission from time in purgatory. The cost of indulgences helped underpin some of the finances of the Catholic Church in Europe. Another sign of the interweaving of Church and society and also of Church and state in Margery's book was the fear of the Lollards. The Lollards were precursors of the later Protestant Reformation, and were seen as dangerous heretics. Lollardy could threaten the stability not only of Catholic doctrine but also of the political structures of the state. Margery was unjustly suspected of being a Lollard; the Lollards were seen as a destabilizing menace, and Margery's extraordinary behaviour pointed towards heterodoxy not unlike that of the Lollards.

These vignettes from Margery's life, and subsequently from the civic life of Bishop's Lynn, are but a few examples of the complex interweaving of religion with everyday life. Many of the distinctions that might be made in the twenty-first century about sacred and secular would simply not have applied or made sense in pre-Reformation England. Although Margery is something of an extreme example of mediaeval piety, with her somewhat neurotic patterns of prayer and her wish to end conjugal relations with her husband – not to mention her unbearable bouts of crying and tears within and outside the liturgy of the Church – still many of her perceptions are typical of her times. The economy and the polity of Church and society were at times virtually seamless and fed each other richly. This phenomenon has been superbly and graphically illustrated in Eamon Duffy's intriguing picture of life both on the cusp of and during the English Reformation in just one tiny North Devon village.[2]

One aspect of this interwoven life to which Duffy adverts is the profusion of images of saints which were clearly at the heart of the devotional life of Sir Christopher Trychay, the parish priest. Not only were there the 'statutory' (so to speak) images of the Virgin and St George, patron of England, but alongside there were saints of a more exotic hue. These included St Loy or St Eligius, the patron of smiths and carters, who was a favourite in the south west of England. Also there were St Anne, the mother of the Virgin and the Sunday Christ, a 'Man of Sorrows' portrayal of Jesus. Perhaps most important of all was Sir Christopher's initiation of the cult of a local saint within his church at Morebath. Both Devon and especially Cornwall still have a rich harvest of saints honoured in a very specific locality. In Cornwall these include St Ivo, St Piran, St Winwaloe and many others. In North Devon, St Nectan is remembered at Hartland and St Urith at Chittlehampton.

It was, however, to Exeter and St Sidwell that Trychay turned. St Sidwell's body lay in a church dedicated to her, outside the city of Exeter. Trychay's introduction of this image added a specificity and local interest and devotion to the images honoured in Morebath Church. One of the key points that Duffy makes, both with regard to St Sidwell's image and those of St Loy, the Virgin and others, was the way in which the maintenance and beautification of these images was completely and utterly dovetailed into the life of the local community. One indicator of this is the means by which the finance for maintenance of the images was provided. So, in 1528, William Potter at Poole left a hive of bees, (which John Morsse had managed for him) to the altar of Jesus and St Sidwell, and he included the wax. The legacy read:

> to maintain a lamp burning before the figure of Jesus and before St Sidwell every principal feast in the year, to burn from the first evensong [i.e. first vespers of the feast] until high Mass be done the next day.[3]

Elsewhere Sir Christopher records another gift – this time from Joan Hillyer of Brampton – with some clear enthusiasm:

> Upon which candlestick she doth maintain a taper before St Sidwell trimmed with flowers to burn them every high

and principal feast: this she doth intend to maintain while
she liveth, by the grace of God.[4]

Nevertheless, this focus upon legacies and gifts does not fully
do justice to the complex interrelationship between faith and
everyday life which existed at that time, although the hive of bees
offers a hint. The gift of bees points to a continuing source
of revenue for maintenance of the cult, and this extended more
widely into the local economy. So, earlier in his account, Duffy
refers to the sheep, which were both an elemental part of the
village's agriculture and also formed part of the church flock.
This flock was integral to the annual economic well-being of
Morebath church. It is worth stepping back a pace or two to view
the broader tapestry which Duffy describes in the tiny village
of Morebath.

We have already seen that in the parish church there were
a number of images of the saints. The images not only had to
be both maintained and beautified; it was also important that a
light should be kept burning before them. These lights were
themselves maintained from a series of so-called 'stores'. A store
was a devotional fund, and it was supported by some form of
'commercial' backing, perhaps through the profits on ale brewed
locally, by individual bequests and gifts, or by small flocks of
sheep kept for this very purpose. Generally each store had its
own warden. St Anthony's store had two wardens elected annually, and the income came from the store's flock of sheep. Any
surplus income gained by the store would go into the High Warden's
(churchwarden's) stock and so be available more widely for the
expenses of the parish.[5]

In the late 1530s, as the Henrician Reformation (the first of
a series of English Reformations)[6] got underway, so this began
to impinge upon the ecclesiastical economics of the parish of
Morebath, and indeed upon all the ancient ecclesiastical parishes
in England. So in 1539 all the church flocks were assimilated
to the store of Our Lady.[7] In Morebath the system relating to
the church sheep was particularly detailed and sophisticated. In
principle the sheep were distributed one to a household. This
gave personal responsibility for the sheep to all the people of
the parish, and meant therefore that the economics which supported the devotional life of the parish were spread evenly and

demanded something of everyone in the locality. The existence of these flocks of sheep, then, both underpinned the financial support of the parish church and also drew every single person into a woven tapestry which made church and community of a piece. Issues about the boundaries between sacred and secular effectively did not exist.

Duffy presses the point further still. Annually there were sheep counts to make certain that the economics of the parish were functioning effectively. These counts were a yearly means of ensuring that the obligations of each individual were fulfilled and that these obligations were part of a mutual responsibility within the parish. The accounts were set out in a standard form which has the feel of both litany and ritual as one reads it. Here is a brief extract which gives the feel of these remarkable counts:

> John Morsse hath in his keeping a wether, which has been sold. John Goodman's wether is sold and he hath in his keeping another lamb that came from John at count. John Waters has none of this store, but he hath two ewes of St Anthony's store. Joan at Poole's wether is sold and now she hath no store, as yet. John at Burston a wether. Jekyn Isac a ewe and no lamb this year.

As the priest accounted for the flocks and the individual sheep in this way, so he both brought together the economics of the parish and wove into this a practical ritual which related directly to the devotions of the faithful and to the focus of the community's religious life in the parish church. The priest assembled these ritual accounts not only on his own behalf but also for the wardens. So priest, wardens and the entire community were held together by this practical but, to modern eyes, curious ritual relating to the church sheep. We can now begin to see just how interrelated was the everyday life of the community, its economics and its religious observance.

None of this necessarily tells us anything of the day-to-day, week-by-week religious devotions of the village populace. It does not necessarily demonstrate that village churches were packed Sunday by Sunday in the mediaeval period. Indeed, mediaeval historians have sometimes been uncertain of the regular devotions of all within the community. Sir Richard Southern, in responding to comments about the modern breakdown in religious devotion, was keen to argue for an element of agnosticism, or even scepticism, about packed churches in halcyon mediaeval days.[8] Nevertheless, these practices do indicate a pattern of life whereby religion and the quotidian demands of labour and economics were held together in one woven tapestry.

This is one of the points which Duffy extrapolates from his fascinating piece of 'micro-research' into the historical background of the English Reformation. Henry VIII's Reformation was, of course, as much political and economic as it was religious. The king had much to gain from the dissolution of the monasteries and the appropriation of their wealth to the Crown. The process of reformation had, however, still more sweeping effects upon the pattern of life across England. The break-up of the vast lands earlier held by religious had its own impact. The patterns of education, poor relief and large-scale farming were broken down and fragmented. The monastic granges went to the Crown or to private individuals, or sometimes were retained by cathedrals and other ecclesiastical peculiars. This had its own effect upon the economics and community life of the nation.

The series of reformations in England throughout the sixteenth century, however, also had an impact through the break-up of community life and religious devotion described above. In 1542 injunctions were announced which barred all lights and candles anywhere in church except for two candles on the high altar. Furthermore, all stocks, funds and stores used in the past to maintain lamps and candles were now to be put into the poor box; a certain proportion might be used to maintain the fabric of the church building itself. Commissioners were appointed and sent out with articles of enquiry (they operated rather like latter-day draconian archdeacons) to implement and enforce these new measures.

The impact of these changes on Morebath and other ecclesiastical parishes was radical. In 1547 the remarkable ritual of the sheep count was carried out for the last time.[9] No longer did the sheep formally belong to the store established to maintain the lights. The entire flock of church sheep was sold for the knock-down price of 42 shillings for 17 beasts. Sir Christopher Trychay, the incumbent, bought the church bees. Church ales were also prohibited; here the cool winds of Puritanism had begun to blow. These changes had, of course, severe effects upon the economics of parish churches, and financial crises soon loomed. In the West Country the production of ale had been an important source of revenue to parish churches.

*

At this point the different strands of the argument need to be separated. First of all, the economics. The evidence set out by Duffy and others does not somehow suggest that the collapse of pre-Reformation devotions had an all-embracing effect upon rural economics. Church flocks were only one small part of the mediaeval rural scene. The great wool trade of Norfolk and Suffolk, for example, was not directed to the provision of images for local saints and the maintenance of lights before them. The existence of the great 'wool churches' at Salle and Worstead, Lavenham and Long Melford is a rather different testimony to the affluence of wool merchants and their patronage of the local church. On the wider economic scene, the collapsing of mediaeval devotions had merely a passing effect upon the trade in wool and the keeping of sheep.

Second, the financial crisis which hit the parishes was one direct economic effect of the progress of the Reformation. This came from a number of different directions. The abolition of images meant the dispersal of church flocks and of hives of bees. Prohibition of the brewing of ale hit hard at the economics of parishes in certain parts of the country. Then the suppression of chantries also had its effects. Chantries had meant that the great and the good could leave money for the establishment of an altar (and often a chapel) in a church or cathedral – or sometimes even on a bridge, as at Rotherham and Wakefield in Yorkshire – so that priests would regularly say mass for them and pray for their souls. The endowment of such chantries, again, was an important element in the economics of parish churches.

There is no doubting the financial crisis effected by all these changes, but these were by no means the most far-reaching effects of the change wrought by the series of reformations in the sixteenth century. These more far-reaching effects were only partially economic and may well have contributed to the complex process which is sometimes described as 'secularization'. This term is itself now to a large degree discredited, even in the world of sociologists of religion. Nevertheless a clear sociological shift occurred. Perhaps the process about to be described here is better described as 'the alienation of religion from everyday life'. It is not one single process, but rather a series of different incidents, events and factors that have in different ways sundered a religious understanding of human existence from the ordinary and practical patterns of everyday life. We shall encounter this again in a later period as urbanization and the industrial revolution altered irrevocably the pattern of people's lives; hints of this have already been given in our introductory chapter.

Here, however, the context is different. Duffy's fascinating analysis has indicated how the place of the parish church in pre-Reformation England was inextricably intermeshed with the community, and with those occupations which were at the heart of the rural economy. Let us begin with these occupations and their contribution to this integrated pattern of life which abhors division between sacred and secular. Although it would be facile to argue that the keeping of sheep and bees were the only industries or occupations which gave life and prosperity to mediaeval England, it is clear that symbolically they were crucial. Both of them were rooted in the natural patterns of rural life. Bees were significant for honey, for the production of mead and for wax: food, drink and light. The wax had immediate uses in the devotional life of the Church. The woollen industry was an essential part of the economy of mediaeval England and had been the source of prosperity in some of the richest parts of the country. The fact that the life of the Church was clearly linked into these two rural occupations was more than symbolic. It spoke of an integration of those things which sustained both body and soul. Indeed, it effectively spoke to the identity of both individual and community. This would not have occurred to people at a self-conscious level but instead ran far more deeply than that.

Communities are so often distinguished by those activities which have given them shape. We have seen this very starkly during the past quarter of a century, with the collapse of deep mining in the coal industry. Few would deny the direness of conditions for those who work underground. Even with modern developments in mining technology it can surely be argued that the moment when no human being has ever again to descend into the earth to mine coal must be a triumphant one. Nevertheless, despite the despicable conditions underground and the known effects upon people's health, the industry itself gave identity and purpose to these communities. The immediate aftermath of the collapse of the industry has been a demonstration of a lack of sense of purpose. Communities no longer have any clear feeling of a central aim; there is a feeling of rudderlessness.

It is likely that in pre-Reformation England (and, indeed, later) the woollen industry was similarly defining of rural life. While the Reformation itself did not remove the woollen industry, nevertheless the dislocation of popular piety from everyday life, the removal of the link between sheep – the symbol of commerce and livelihood and the daily means of labour – and the pattern of parish church devotion and economics will have been profound. It was not simply the abolition of a particular mode of piety, although that would have been traumatic in itself. Instead it was the dismantling of a pattern of life which brought together the parish church, popular devotion, the priest and the stuff of everyday life that took a first step in distancing the people of the land from the faith that had sustained them. Furthermore, this change effectively came by state edict and social revolution, and not by a natural and comprehensible process of evolution. Landmarks which had cemented together priest and people, religious devotion and the land, had been sundered by political decree.

These changes were more significant still, since they presaged the separation of community from faith. Here begins a long process of dissolving this mutuality of society and devotion. Every member of the community had been caught up into this process and this way of life; the ritual of the sheep count speaks of this most powerfully. There was a very obvious practical matrix that stood at the heart of the community's religious life. Sheep were tended; this provided the money to support the devotion; the devotees were brought into the Church through the pattern of work and mutual interdependence and relationship that existed. As the impact of the Reformation changes began to be felt, so much of this matrix was effectively dismantled.

With images, and their accompanying lights, coming under the ban, so the church flocks were wound up and sold. Not only did this remove a regular source of income, it also made otiose the annual sheep count. The loss of this ritual removed the framework which had kept the members of the community together and mutually interdependent in their part in the structures of the parish church. Even if the pattern of images and lights may now appear antique, this pattern of life rooted faith in the practical. Devotion to the Virgin, to St Loy, to St Sidwell, and indeed to Jesus, was not an abstract matter. Such devotion called out of individuals – and the community as a whole – practical action. Through this exchange, the village was caught up into the cult and the story which lay behind it. Ancillary devotions slotted into this, including Marian devotions, prayers for those who had died, and local cults like those of St Sidwell, St Nectan and the Cornish saints.

Alongside all these changes, other external signs were soon to be forbidden. The tolling of knells and the wearing of black copes by the clergy were two signs to be ruled out of court. These changes had a rather different effect. This time the shifts would be less sociological in their impact and more directly related to the communication and comprehension of the faith. The most rigorous Protestants were keen to concentrate purely on the word. The drama and colour of mediaeval Catholicism was to be purged. Eventually this would result in the clearance of all images, the destruction of roods and rood screens, and the desecration of stained glass. There are links here, however, with the other changes. Just as the removal of images had spelt the end of the old parish church economy, and also an unavoidable loss of practical involvement of the people, so worship itself would be sheared of its drama. Again, there was a move from the story enacted and painted to the story told in words. A cerebral and conceptual faith would not retain the same holding power on the minds and hearts of the people.

As has already been hinted, however, the English Reformation was not one single, smooth and unrelenting process. After the increasingly serious strictures of Henry's reign, there followed the most severe Protestantism in the English Church during the brief reign of the child king, Edward VI. Recent studies leave us in no doubt of the Protestant intentions of Edward, his protectors and Thomas Cranmer, his archbishop.[10] It is tempting to look to the reign of Queen Mary for a remission in these shifts towards a thoroughly Protestant ordered polity, and of course there was a remission, but only in the direction of a 'reformed Catholicism'. Cardinal Reginald Pole became Archbishop of Canterbury and papal jurisdiction was restored. Many of the reforms, however, had gone too far to allow for a total reversal. The monasteries had been dissolved. Mary did not attempt to reintroduce the chantries. The former agrarian patterns of church flocks and sheep counts had also gone too far to allow a restoration of old patterns. Gifts and legacies now paid for the re-introduction of images on a fairly wide basis, but this was a long way from restoring the integrated rural piety and economy of pre-Reformation days. Indeed, one might even argue that a dependence upon the legacies and gifts of the rich and great meant a shift towards the Church in England becoming a church of the aristocracy and landed classes. Certainly, the crucial matrix which we have described – a matrix uniting the entire community and integrating religion and everyday life – could not have been restored during the brief Marian interlude. Elizabeth would opt for a Protestantism founded on that established by her father and stepbrother but distanced from the radical Puritan tendencies which would have opted for a full-blooded Protestant English Church. Romish plots were suppressed fiercely, and England became far from the religiously tolerant land that claims often suggest it always has been!

*

This dramatic revolution, effected in this series of English reformations, set the scene for a new way of the people of England to relate to both the Church and the Christian faith. Cranmer's ideal had been to provide the new materials and tools for a popular piety. This lay behind the simplified pattern of offices. It was also in theory to be a declericalized piety, but Cranmer's own plans, and later the Elizabethan Settlement, as it came to be called, made this impossible in any radical sense. The offices could only be made mandatory for clergy. Hence instead the Church of England became one of only three churches across the world to continue the ancient threefold pattern of bishop, priest and deacon; it remained an unquestionably clerically ordered church.

But what were the seminal effects of the dissolution of the pre-Reformation matrix? How did the disappearance of the church flocks and parish beehives in the local church also affect the relationship of the people to their faith? It is impossible to answer this conclusively; sufficient sociological evidence cannot be assembled 450 years on. Even so, some reflections can be made. It seems likely, for example, that the collapse of the old framework, the unravelling of the tapestry of economics, daily life and piety, has been of considerably more profound significance than the removal of the images themselves. The piety which surrounded these devotions would largely disappear, except in recusant circles; the recusants were those families which kept within the jurisdiction of the Pope and emerged as traditional Roman Catholic observants, as the laws of toleration allowed them so to do. But new patterns of holiness would arrive. The religious consciousness of humanity is very rich and endlessly creative. Whether it be Lutheran hymns, the piety of the Caroline Divines or the writings of the Puritans, new pieties would arise and enrich the treasury of the universal Church.

It was the other effects of the removal of the images, however, which had the most devastating effect. For their removal meant also the end of the means by which they were funded and maintained. This resulted in the disintegration of a tapestry and network which held all the people of the parishes within the structure of a common piety and together in a broader community. The matrix would never be rebuilt and would perforce result in the people – and notably the ordinary people – of the land relating to the Christian faith in quite different ways. It is not within the compass of this book to trace this story in detail through the Puritan Revolution to the seventeenth-century restoration. Nonetheless, at no point during the ensuing centuries was the 'sociological fabric' repaired. All that would follow would be structured on the very different foundations of a new order. Even the footings of the old order had disappeared for ever.

It would be an exercise in archaeological and historical fantasy to attempt to rebuild the pre-Reformation world of English religion. Of course, the use of images survives within Roman Catholicism, albeit within the context of the Vatican II reforms, and then in a quite different way in the honouring of icons in Orthodoxy. In Catholic Anglicanism the use of images has also survived to a degree; statues of Our Lady and of other saints are still honoured in Anglo-Catholic churches. Nowhere in this

country, however, have the structures which went with mediaeval religion survived. When one enters a glorious mediaeval
English church, of which thousands survive, (there are more than
400 in Norfolk alone), one wonders how such buildings were
built and maintained, often in tiny communities. Sometimes it
was the patronage or the wealth of a particular industry like
wool. Often it was the intricate and integral structure of rural
life and the piety it fed which allowed these places to prosper.

Instead, then, of indulging in the fantasy of restoring a lost
framework tapestry and structure, is there anything that can be
learnt from the disintegration of this remarkable world? Did the
disappearance of this world form the backcloth to other key
moments when the Church in England somehow further lost
touch with the heart and the energizing spirits of the people of
the country? This is the question with which to end this brief
analysis. It will be a contributing question to the broader canvas
that will eventually emerge. From that canvas, might we learn
something of how people may be reconnected with a lively faith
in this extraordinarily contrasting age?

3

Hearts strangely cooled?

It is this English Church, snug and smug among the hed-
gerows that has done it. That is the astonishing thing. It
has thrown feelers out so far and wide. It has overleaped
the paddock fence. It has flung out its frontier line. It has
set sail with every wind that blows, and planted its feet
on every shore that the ocean washes. Who would have
dreamed it of her? She hardly believes it herself. She finds
it difficult to remember as she sits tied up in Elizabethan red
tape, and smothered under the conventions of Establishment,
and fat with dignities, and very scant of breath. Yet it is all
true. For here were the adventurers whom she had sent out,
trooping home to din the story into her dim, deaf ears.[1]

So wrote Henry Scott Holland, reflecting upon the worldwide
Pan-Anglican Congress of 1908. His reflections were, of course,
upon the spread of Anglicanism across the world; Robert Runcie
used frequently and appositely to say that after Roman Catholicism, Anglicanism is the form of Christianity most widely spread
across the globe. Scott Holland's words read alternately as com-
placent and perceptive. But would such a snapshot be drawn of
the Church of England earlier on, in the late sixteenth century
or indeed in the seventeenth or eighteenth centuries? Would it
still feel as expansive and as generous in spirit? Might not the
following verse have been a more accurate perception, at least
for a significant minority of recusant Catholics or Dissenters, of
various sorts and conditions?

> They drew a circle that shut me out –
> Heretic, rebel, a thing to flout,
> But love and I had the wit to win –
> We drew a circle that took them in.[2]

Intentionally, even within the provisions of the Elizabethan Settlement, they certainly 'drew a circle to shut people out'. The English have traditionally prided themselves on their tolerance and sense of inclusivity. That was not how things would have felt during the late sixteenth century. In his magisterial analysis of the European Reformation, Diarmaid MacCulloch presents the figures for executions and paints a frightening picture of Elizabethan persecution. He notes: 'In fact England judicially murdered more Roman Catholics than any other country in Europe, which puts English pride in national tolerance in an interesting perspective.'[3]

It would be well over a century before the impact of moves towards toleration would become clear. Even the Glorious Revolution of 1688 and the writers of the English Enlightenment – John Locke and others – would not lead to instant toleration. It was not until 1829 that the Catholic Emancipation Act passed through Parliament. Fellowships at the two ancient universities remained firmly attached to ordination in the Church of England until the second half of the nineteenth century. Intolerance of nonconformity remained a characteristic of many Church of England dignitaries into the late nineteenth and early twentieth centuries. William Butler, the celebrated vicar of Wantage and from 1885 to 1896 Dean of Lincoln, writing in his parish journal in 1876 noted: 'Churchmen, trying by all legitimate means to win Dissenters and the careless of whom, alas we have very many among us . . . hardly manifested the much admired English "virtue of toleration".'[4]

This may be the root of an adage still frequently picked up in popular culture: 'Two subjects should never be discussed over a pint in the pub: religion and politics.'

This adage has become virtually a cliché, but it is partly the very mixture of religion and politics during and since the Reformation that has provided such a toxic or explosive atmosphere, and the background to such a cliché. Such an antagonistic context could hardly be guaranteed to win the hearts of the English people, even by those who favour combative management theory. This potent mixture of politics and religion did not dissipate or fade away. William Laud, Archbishop of Canterbury during the reign of King Charles I, was keen to restore collective sacramental and spiritual observances within the Church of England. During the 1620s and 1630s, Laudian religion, combined with Charles I's belief in the 'divine right of kings', provoked new and different explosive situations. Indeed, this formed the seedbed for the conflict of the 1640s and for the radical movements of the Commonwealth period. Both Laud's personality and the policies which he pursued (directly derivative of his own religious convictions) helped inflame an increasingly divided culture. There is no doubting the fact that religion and strongly held but divergent religious beliefs were one, if not the only, essential driving force leading to the English Civil War. In her survey of the period 1642–60, Judith Maltby quotes John Morrill on the Stuart Church.

> Between 1640 and 1642 the Church of England collapsed, its leaders reviled and discredited, its structures paralysed, its practices if not yet prescribed, at least inhibited. In the years that followed yet worse was to befall it.[5]

Morrill goes on to point to the fresh shoots that would spring up, but still there is no doubting the religious turmoil of the years encompassed by the Civil War and the Commonwealth. These catastrophic religious experiences unquestionably left their marks in different ways on the population of the country and upon individuals too. Maltby mentions Clement Spelman, a Norfolk gentleman who bemoans the trouble of these two decades. He sees the ills of the times relating directly to the seizure of church property by the Crown. Here once again we see echoes of the shift in society and Church caused by changes in polity and in the deep structures of local communities. It is not the same as Morebath, but there are clear resonances. Patterns within society were changed irrevocably and this had a direct impact upon the relationships of the Christian religion to the daily life of the people. This process would of course accelerate and be magnified in the years after the death of the king in 1649. The Commonwealth period saw the religious life of the nation expressed in quite different polities, in both the secular and the spiritual realms. The common, almost folklore-like references to horses being stabled by the New Model Army in virtually every large church and cathedral in the land combine with present-day comment that divisions between villages reach back to them being on different sides of the conflict during the

Puritan Revolution. On a more scholarly level, even a glance at the very few churches to be built in the Commonwealth period indicates the different polity or tradition represented by Cromwell's Puritan party.[6]

So, during the Commonwealth years Protestants organized themselves into groups which would assume a permanence outside the circle of the established Church. It was such groups that would result eventually in the variety of dissenting assemblies that we now know as Baptists, Congregationalists and Independents. This movement was accompanied by the rise of radical groups who were infected with millenarian beliefs; it was clear to such groups that they were living in the 'Last Days'. Revolutionary groups of the twentieth century frequently sought their inspiration from these extreme Puritan sects. Some saw them as proto-Marxists. So the 'Ranters' might see the future in terms of the overthrow of all spiritual and worldly laws. Diarmaid MacCulloch points to some who made gestures of what he calls 'exotic blasphemy'. People ran naked down the street and engaged in joyous tobacco smoking. Among other Ranters were those who sought out an 'inner light'. This both harked back to earlier movements of the 1530s and also found echo later on in the development of the Society of Friends or Quakers.[7]

George Fox, who inspired the foundation of the Friends, was also working in this period. But Fox, radical as he was, was concerned to channel these currents of thoughts into worthwhile spiritual paths. Eventually the Quakers proved to be one of the few radical groups to survive from the millenarian explosion. On the contrasting and most secular side stood the Diggers, whose aim was to dig up common land and set up communities that would hold all in common. Despite the popular view of Cromwell as a radical, the ultimate tendency in the Commonwealth period was more conservative. Even Roman Catholics were less persecuted, as indeed were nobility who hankered after a continuity of episcopal polity and worship. Nevertheless the fragmenting impact of these changes was here to stay. The sense of 'one Christendom' or at the very least a continuing catholic Christianity, in the sense of one united universal Church, was lost for ever. More than that, even a national Church of England was inevitably undermined and, despite the strictures of the Clarendon Code, enacted during the Restoration period of the 1660s, this could not reverse the fragmentation that had occurred. Persecution ironically had the opposite effect to that which was intended, the outlawed groups grew stronger in their defiance. All this took its toll. MacCulloch notes:

> In the new situation, the Church of England became a vast federation of parishes, with virtually no control structure apart from a London committee known as the Triers, set up to examine candidates for the ministry and drawn from all shades of Protestant opinion. As a result, parishes could go their own way, which usually meant a personal adaptation of the supposedly illegal Book of Common Prayer in a Protestant direction.[8]

Once again, further fragmentation was the result. The intention of 'Common Prayer' which stood at the heart of the Elizabethan prayer book was defeated by the tendencies towards disintegration within the national Church. The Restoration of Charles II in 1660 was remarkable in its capacity to reverse so many of the tendencies of the so-called 'Interregnum' between the first Charles and his son.

Nevertheless the desire to draw tighter boundaries around the re-established Church did in itself institutionalize the divisions that had arisen. Significant numbers of clergy no longer found it possible to remain within the Church of England. Archbishop Sancroft, Charles II's archbishop, had an ironic career. He was one of those who helped create a more watertight Church of England and in the process created, from the Puritans and other Protestants, the new identity of Dissent.[9] With the arrival of William III, Sancroft's High Church principles led him and other bishops into refusing to take the oath of allegiance to the new king, and thus he himself became an 'Establishment Dissenter'. He did so alongside a number of other so-called 'non-juring' bishops. The Clarendon Code, including the Five-Mile Act, the Corporation Act, the Conventicle Act and the Test Act, reinforced the new boundaries around the established Church. Effectively they made the 1660 Act of Uniformity more excluding still than the Tudor acts of the same title. The exclusiveness and persecution which followed helped form Dissent in contrast to the established Church of England. It was the Glorious Revolution of 1688, the deposition of James II and the accession of William and Mary, that, with the 1689 Toleration Act, set England out on the long march towards a more flexible polity.

By now, however, an irreversible fragmentation had occurred and the toleration that would slowly develop would, in an ironic way, institutionalize this fragmentation. There is no doubt that with regard to the political development of England, and ultimately Britain, this new fragmented polity would ultimately be a most positive movement. It offered alternatives. Indeed, it would presage other shifts, philosophically with the writings of John Locke and others, and eventually it would lead to the emancipation of Roman Catholics in the early nineteenth century. The much-vaunted English virtue of toleration would eventually spring from this acceptance of a fragmentation borne both of a Puritan revolution and of a restored monarchy. The open-weave society that would result would lead both to a more varied spectrum of polity on the religious scene and also to a democracy with a capacity to hear the voices of both Establishment and Dissent within a broader political matrix.

Even so, this partial disintegration would leave its mark on religious observance in England and would have an impact on the effectiveness of the churches in 'winning souls for Christ'. First of all, religious rivalry in itself can easily undermine the power of human consciousness to engage with religious belief. If such belief is about the existence of some objective ultimate reality, then how does this assumed objectivity engage with the human subjectivity that appears to be manifested by such a great variety of Christian religious observance? Second, any sense of a common fabric of culture is destroyed by such fragmentation. Christopher Dawson, in an earlier generation, made frequent reference to the effects of the Reformation on European culture. At one point, he writes:

> The theocratic unity of mediaeval Christendom was destroyed, and Europe became a society of sovereign states in which the temporal power of the prince either abolished or severely limited the spiritual power of the universal Church. From the religious point of view this loss of Christian unity was a tragedy from which Christendom has never recovered.[10]

At the heart of his analysis, then, lay the realization that the common religious culture which framed European civilization, in a certain sort of way, was swept away with the fragmenting effects of the sixteenth-century Reformation. Putting on one side the macro effects of this, notably with the dissolution of the monasteries in England, and much later with the ravaging of monasticism across Europe by Napoleon, there was also an accelerating micro effect. This began with the movements described in Morebath, which increased, as persecution drove out Dissenters both in Elizabethan times and following the Puritan Revolution. Indeed, that revolution itself magnified these disintegrative processes. The effect of this fragmentation on the micro level was to dissolve any common culture and common mission in villages, and towns – and eventually in suburbs – as the industrial revolution moved apace.

There was a third shift that we have already identified and which needs further extrapolation. This was the sharper sense of boundaries to the established Church effected through the legal and cultural responses which followed the restoration of the monarchy in 1660. These sharper boundaries made plain the existence of Dissent, both in terms of the newly established Protestant groupings: Baptists, Congregationalists, Friends, Independents, and indeed in terms of the recusant Roman Catholic community. This new situation and the very existence of Dissent, as it became defined, could not but have an impact on the 'social psychology' of the Church of England. There was a sense in which its identity became unavoidably more self-conscious. Its own divisions, following the non-juring response to the accession of the dual monarchy of William and Mary, may have contributed further to this self-consciousness. Whatever our analysis of that response might be, there is no doubting this growth of a new social psychology within the established Church. The effects of this would be more clearly seen in its response to the work of George Whitefield and John Wesley and what would eventually emerge as the Methodist movement. Ultimately, the Church of England found itself incapable of containing this new upsurge of spiritual energy. How did this happen and how would it impinge upon the hearts of the English people?

*

The origins of Methodism and its relationship to the eighteenth-century English evangelical revival have been rehearsed in detail in a variety of histories of the period. The key issue within this present analysis concerns how the rise of Methodism might have had an effect upon the hearts of the English people and their response to the Christian gospel. In the light of a dawning religious toleration, what was the contribution of Methodism and how did the Church of England respond to it? Was there at this point an opportunity for a healing in the fragmentation of English religious culture, and did this offer a new hope in touching people's hearts?

There seems little doubt that the initial response to these new signs of toleration was an apprehensiveness on the part of churchmen within the established Church of England. Would this new freedom not open the floodgates to every form of dissident or wild belief? Might it not even lead to apathy or a lack of interest in religion? This second question does indeed provoke interesting reflections in the light of twentieth- and early twenty-first-century experience of a falling away from Christian belief through a lack of interest rather than through a deliberate hostility. Using the language of Wesley's renowned conversion experience in Aldergate Street, the stirrings of the English Enlightenment even suggested that the fear was that the hearts of many might be strangely *cooled* by the bracing winds of toleration. In fashionable circles, free-thinking was spreading. Furthermore, the undoubted religious convictions of Isaac Newton and John Locke respectively (the leading scientist and philosopher of the early English Enlightenment) were hardly those convictions that underpinned the existence of a redeeming interventionist God, in the most full-blooded understanding of the Christian tradition. The atmosphere of deism was already beginning to filter into the air.

Furthermore, the spread of toleration was also making possible the flourishing of every form of dissenting religious group. The established Church was already showing signs of insecurity, if not paranoia. Joseph Trapp, an Anglican priest, noted that 'all manner of wickedness both in principles and in practice, abounds among us to a degree unheard of since Christianity was in being'.[11]

Among these 'dissident groups,' however, the position of Methodism was unique. The impulses of the 'Holy Club' and the earliest supporters of Methodism (as it became known) were those of reform and a new passion for the gospel within the established Church of England. Although one of its founding fathers, George Whitefield, was a Calvinist, John Wesley himself had encountered very different influences. His encounter with the Moravian tradition and his subsequent embracing of an Arminian theology and spirituality meant that his own cradle Anglicanism could happily engage with the broader elements within the established Church. There was no need to move in the direction of sectarian dissent. Arminianism left a far greater scope for free will and affirmed God's will that all should be saved. It stood foursquare in opposition to the Calvinistic doctrine of predestination. Both of Charles I's archbishops – Laud at Canterbury and Richard Neile at York – were Arminians and the theological shift which this presaged shifted the ethos of the Church of England. The sacramentalism to which Wesley was committed was part and parcel of this Arminianism. All this, then, augured well for the established Church being able to take the enthusiasm represented by Wesley and his followers into its system. Furthermore, both Wesley and the Calvinist Whitefield were themselves Anglican priests.

There were very good reasons why the Church of England would do well to embrace the Methodist movement – for that was what it was, not a sect or an emergent denomination. Chief among the reasons for embracing the Methodist revival was that it responded so immediately to the needs of the time, for both religiously and socially the English people were ready to be receptive to the Christian message couched in the terms that Wesley offered it, and delivered with the passion with which his own conversion had inspired him. Undoubtedly there were 'dry' elements within the eighteenth-century Church of England and there also lingered a Calvinism to which Whitefield would have been attracted, and which would be rekindled by some elements in the Church of England's own evangelical revival later in the century. There was also, however, the need to make contact with the poor, the needy and the neglected. The established nature of the Church of England, and by dint of this its identification with those laws which placed Dissenters outside the established religious order, meant an obvious link with the 'great and the good', an identification with the powerful, the ruling class. Furthermore, the established Church, early on, failed manifestly to respond effectively to the growing numbers of urban poor as the industrial revolution got underway.

Here Wesley was in his element. By choice he went among the poor and knew them. He not only preached among the poor but also raised money to buy necessities, even opening a dispensary for the many poor who were also sick. He founded a home for widows and set up the eighteenth-century equivalent of a mutual society aimed at offering loans to those in particular need; it was almost the first version of what we now describe as 'credit unions'. Wesley saw poverty as a social problem with which government should engage. Even so, it would be facile and misjudged to see Wesley as the systematic initiator of serious social reform. Henry Rack notes:

> It was poverty and the related question of wealth which most excited his concern, leading him to practical solutions as well as to one or two excursions into what contemporaries called 'political economy'.[12]

It does seem to be the case that once again his attitude to poverty and to the poor derives both from his Arminian doctrinal background and from his extraordinary knowledge of the social circumstances of such a wide spectrum of the people of eighteenth-century England. Arminianism's conviction that God's love is poured out equally upon all requires the Christian to respond to everyone, but particularly to those in need – he spoke with an irascible intolerance of the ostentation of the rich. His remarkable peripatetic ministry of preaching meant that he encountered 'all sorts and conditions of people' unknown to many at the time. Conservative estimates put his travelling down as at least a quarter of a million miles in his lifetime. This has to allow, too, for the fact that transport was entirely on foot or on horseback.

So Wesley's real concern for the poor, his missionary preaching zeal, his concern for holiness and perfection, offered a complementary ministry to that of the Church of England in many of its manifestations. This, combined with his Arminian theological underpinning, seems to argue for an alliance or, better still, an influencing of the ministry of the established Church which would have offered a more comprehensive pastoral care and mission for the people of eighteenth-century England. 'Comprehensiveness' is a term which, in the twentieth century, was often embraced warmly by Anglicans to describe the breadth of different theological traditions exemplified within one Church. It is doubtful now whether this comprehensiveness can even be claimed in quite this way theologically; divisions appear to run deeper than some of those things which are held in common. However that might be, the boast of a comprehensive coverage, through parish ministry, by a national Church, may always have been more apparent than real. This can be seen perhaps more starkly as one compares the respective ministries of Anglicans (admittedly a term of later coinage) and Methodists, as they would become known in the eighteenth century. If Wesley's initiative could help broaden the base of the established Church's ministry, why did Anglicans not take the opportunity to embrace this new spiritual flowering? After all, it sprang from roots within its own community when it was nourished by an Arminian nutrient already flowing richly within the bloodstream of the Church of England.

It would be easy to place the blame fairly and squarely upon the sclerotic attitudes and personalities of the established Church, but on its own this would be profoundly unfair. Wesley himself made it difficult for Anglicans to embrace that for which he had come to stand. Two matters in particular made it virtually impossible, finally, for the Church of England to embrace Methodism and to avoid schism. Both these issues were actions taken by Wesley in 1784. First of all he designated, through a Deed of Declaration lodged in the Court of Chancery, the appointment of a Conference of 100 specified men which would be his successor. By this action he effectively designated the Methodist Societies as a separate ecclesial institution with its own pre-emptive constitution. The second key action he took related to his fears about proper pastoral care in the American colonies. He feared that the Church of England had done too little in the colonies to set up an effective ministry of the gospel, and this led him to establish a Methodist network there. Even if he had known of Samuel Seabury's consecration by Scottish Episcopal bishops in Aberdeen, later in 1784, this would only have reinforced Wesley's conviction that the English bishops were prepared to do nothing to remedy the situation in the colonies, where regular attendance at the Holy Communion was impossible on account of lack of clergy.

With this in mind, at 6 Dighton Street, Bristol, and without consulting his newly constituted Conference, he ordained Richard Whatcoat and Thomas Vasey as deacons. On the next day they were ordained as presbyters, and at the same service he consecrated the Revd Thomas Coke (who was episcopally ordained) as superintendent. The three then soon set off for a ministry in the colonies. Both these acts were destined to drive a clear division between Methodists and the Church of England, despite Wesley's own loud protests that he 'lived and died in the Church of England'. The first act was effectively the proclamation of a separate ecclesial entity; the second act of ordination flouted the laws and disciplines of the established Church.

Of course it is true that the Church of England itself took no initiative. Rupert Davies makes the point pungently:

> From the first moment of Wesley's itinerant ministry the authorities of the Church of England did precisely nothing, either to prevent a breach or to expel the Methodists. Individual bishops from time to time acted in their own diocese in ways that showed that they approved or disapproved of what Methodists were doing. But of concerted official action there was nothing.[13]

It has been said that the state of the Church of England at that point would have made it difficult to take any concerted action. In the light of this, individual bishops reacted variously. So Bishop Lowth commented: 'Mr Wesley, may I be sitting at your feet in another world.' Bishop Warburton wrote a strong attack on the Methodist doctrine of grace. Bishop Butler's negative response has become almost the stuff of legends: 'Sir, the pretending to extraordinary revelations and gifts of the Holy Ghost is a horrid thing – a very horrid thing.' Archbishop Potter, however, remained on good terms and Bishop Gibson was careful not to condemn. The truth is, of course, that there was no unanimity among the bishops because there were no structures of decision-making that would have allowed for a pronouncement to be made or for negotiations to have been entered. Convocation was in its 140-year recess, so to speak.

In the mid-eighteenth century, the issue of separation was not acute 'on the ground'. It was in the 1750s that pressure really began to build on both sides.[14] Wesley and his followers took less and less notice of parish boundaries, believing that it was essential that they took forward an apostolate to the growing population in the new industrial areas which Wesley believed the ministrations of the Church of England had left virtually untouched. As we shall see later on, the new churches built by the Church of England almost all post-date the growth of Methodism, many such churches being built in the first half of the nineteenth century. Indeed, the foundation of new dioceses is an even more alarming guide. Manchester and Ripon (which then included Leeds, Bradford, Huddersfield, Halifax and Wakefield) were children of the 1830s and 1840s. Wakefield was founded in 1888, and Sheffield and Bradford respectively not until 1914 and 1920; Blackburn was founded in 1926.

The tardiness of the Church of England's response to urbanization and its failure to embrace Methodism as a movement within itself are often seen as indicators of a general ineffectiveness and corruption within the eighteenth-century Church. Recent commentators have, however, begun to correct this simplistic and erroneous analysis.

In his scholarly account of the contribution of the laity in the eighteenth century, W. M. Jacob shows that the Church of England was more alive and in touch with the population than has often been assumed. He argues that religion was still unquestionably the basis of English society. Some have argued for an early date for the secularization of English society; Jacob's analysis of public religious practice, the pursuit of Christian morality, a concern for Christian education and the sheer prevalence of philanthropy and enthusiasm for church-building, however, argue against easy theses of the collapse of Christian culture. He admits that change was in the air, and that the potential for increasing fractures in the Church through toleration must be acknowledged. Furthermore, he does argue that the possibility of a shift to a greater individualism has its roots in this period. He writes: 'The first half of the eighteenth century also saw the beginning of a separation of the Church from people's daily lives and communal activities.'[15]

Noting some further factors which led society in this same general direction, he argues:

These factors were probably quite as important in diminishing the role of the Church in the lives of English people as the attacks on the Church of England's political power, and the slow growth of Enlightenment ideas in England.[16]

Jacob's argument is subtle and multi-layered, and he does not rule out sociological and demographic shifts. He hints at changing patterns in daily work, for example, and suggests that John Wesley's well-known early morning preaching may have been a response to this.[17] Alongside this he points to reform in the support of the less well-off clergy, through Queen Anne's Bounty. He describes the vigorous church-building in the eighteenth century, amply testified to in the buildings of Hawksmoor, James Gibbs and others. Nevertheless, this frenzy of church-building did not keep track with the expansion of the urban areas, as we shall see. Certainly galleries were built in churches to try to keep pace with increasing populations in established urban areas, but there remained vast tracts of newly industrialized England where, in the late eighteenth and early nineteenth centuries, Dissent was more immediate in its response.

It is, however, crucial to remember some of Jacob's key discoveries. First of all, the eighteenth century, building upon the restoration of the Church of England with the accession of Charles II, would mean the triumph of Laudian policies. Second, the Church of England remained a communal church. Indeed, Jacob argues that this was so across the regions of England and across the urban–rural divide. It also appears to have touched all aspects of English society, at least to varying degrees. He notes in passing, 'For nearly everyone God was central to life.'[18] Nevertheless, he also comments:

In retrospect it can be seen that the old order was changing by the middle of the eighteenth century. Patterns of work were changing. People were less willing, or more probably less able, because of their changing work routines to attend weekday services and lectures.[19]

Precisely what effect this had upon churchgoing, especially among what were still described as the 'lower orders', it is difficult to know. Certainly, by the end of the nineteenth century, even in rural areas, adults were lost to the Church except for births, deaths and marriages and at the popular festivals.[20]

It was increasingly the case, then, that the structures of the Church of England were not effectively adapted at this time to the revolutionary nature of demographic change. This meant an ineffective ministry to the new urban poor and, with an unchanging parish system, a lack of flexibility in ministering to people where they now found themselves geographically. It was precisely into this vacuum that Wesley was able to introduce his new networks of voluntary societies, and into which he was able to ride, literally on horseback, with his effective and passionate itinerant ministry of preaching. Still, in so many parts of England there is evidence of his extraordinary energy and passion. From rural Cornwall and Gwennap Pit to Wesley's chapels in Bunhill Fields in London and Bristol, from Norfolk to West Yorkshire – throughout England he preached, and many of the places where he did so still record the presence of this energetic and dynamic preacher. Where an Anglican presence was most sparse, there Methodism most effectively took root. In West Yorkshire and other industrial areas, chapels sprang up in the valleys and on the hillsides ubiquitously; in Cornwall, Methodism effectively became the established religion for almost two centuries, before the accelerated decline of nonconformity in the mid-twentieth century.

These brief reflections on the birth of Methodism and the encounter or lack of encounter between Methodists and the Church of England in the eighteenth century raise issues central to our theme. It could be argued, then, that through the Reformation, the Laudian period and the Puritan Revolution, the Church of England had cumulatively lost the hearts of at least some of the English people. Did not the failure of the established Church to embrace the followers of Methodism – notably in its Wesleyan Arminian form – mark a notable missed opportunity in regard to broadening both the pastoral care of and the preaching of the Christian gospel to the rural poor and to the new rapidly increasing urban poor? It is difficult to answer this in any other manner than the affirmative. Indeed, later in the eighteenth century, the Church of England experienced its own evangelical revival with its own mixture of Calvinism and Arminianism. This was followed by the High Church equivalents, first of all in the Hackney Phalanx and then with the Tractarians and the Oxford Movement. If Methodism had been contained within or embraced by the Church of England, would the religious history of the country have been notably different? After all, Methodism was both revivalist and sacramental.

Interestingly enough, Wesley was himself, alongside his enthusiasm and willingness to set light to church order, an advocate of tolerance. In his famous sermon on the 'Catholic Spirit', he argues that if people agree on belief in God, faith in Jesus Christ, love of God and love of neighbour, they can join not in church government and worship but in love. This catholic spirit does not mean an indifference to all opinions. This leads Henry Rack, one of Wesley's recent biographers, to note:

> It is anachronistic to see Wesley as an ecumenical pioneer in the perspective of the modern ecumenical movement. Nor were his notions of toleration simply the direct fruit of his evangelism. Yet for all his limitations, he was genuinely and passionately opposed to physical persecution. This he owed more than he realised to the benevolent spirit of the eighteenth-century Enlightenment.[21]

This brings us back full circle to the Enlightenment and to the reaction of churchmen to it, both consciously and unconsciously. It also challenges us with questions about the effectiveness of the churches in touching the hearts of people in an increasingly fragmented state. It is too simplistic to lay the blame for the divergence of Methodism and the Church of England at the doors of either of the two individual and emerging institutions, for both were developing in different ways. Nevertheless, the fact of that divergence can ultimately only be one for profound regret. The period of 250 years following the onset of the Reformation would prove to be a period of further fragmentation for Christendom. This fragmentation almost certainly led to a further series of events and movements which would distance the Christian churches from increasing numbers of the English people. Marginalization of the Christian religion, often rather inaccurately described as secularization, is generally seen as a phenomenon of the twentieth century. Even a fairly brief analysis suggests that such alienation has a far longer pedigree. How would the churches seek to respond to these challenges in the nineteenth century, when the process of urbanization changed the nature of English culture?

4

Revivals and refusals

In modern times our relishing of the rural idyll, and our taste for nostalgia, has led to the pastime often known now as 'church-crawling'. Most frequently the locations are rural and mediaeval. Norfolk is a favourite starting point, with the greatest concentration of mediaeval church buildings in Western Europe. There is, however, as much to learn from following circuits of churches often bounded by urban sprawl and even conurbation; buildings which are less evocative aesthetically still have their tale to tell. Let us take an imaginary journey through West Yorkshire, for example. We might begin in the upper Holme Valley, now better known through the medium of television. The church at Holmfirth is eighteenth-century and rather plain. Higher up the valley still is All Saints, Netherthong, built in 1830. Travelling on, and circumnavigating Huddersfield, to the west we encounter Christ Church, Linthwaite, completed just a little earlier, in 1828. Striking further north and west, beyond Halifax, brings us to the small former mill town of Hebden Bridge. St James' is the parish church here, and it was constructed in 1833. Moving back eastwards we can drop into St Martin's at Brighouse; completed in 1830, this is in the heart of former woollen milling country. Still further east takes us into the territory of shoddy mills, and so, for example, to St Paul's, Birkenshaw, completed in 1831. Finally, for now, we make our last call at the church of St John on Dewsbury Moor, which opened its doors in 1827. At this church, Charlotte Brontë was an early worshipper when she moved with Miss Wooler to teach at her new academy, on the edge of Dewsbury. She probably left Roe Head Academy just before Christ Church, Battyeford (now lost by fire) was completed in 1839–40.

Throughout the course of this journey we would encounter numerous disused woollen and shoddy mills of varying shapes and sizes. Sometimes the mills themselves challenge the church buildings for pre-eminence as the most significant and evocative structures within the landscape. Also, however, alongside these Church of England houses of prayer, one will encounter countless smaller chapels and church buildings, signs of the strength of early Methodism and other forms of Dissent. Frequently these buildings – often more modest and austere than their fairly spare Anglican brothers and sisters – will have been built rather earlier. The population of West Yorkshire (or the West Riding as it was then known) grew with great rapidity in the wake of the expansion of the woollen industry. The Church of England was very often late on the scene. Up until then, the moors and farmland of this part of Yorkshire were parcelled out in vast parishes, rooted in the more ancient towns and villages – Almondbury, Halifax, Hartshead, Huddersfield, Kirkheaton and Wakefield itself. Wakefield's great parish church of All Saints is now the cathedral of the diocese. The tardiness of the Church of England in responding to industrial growth and urbanization has appeared to some as a refusal to respond, and to others as a refusal to acknowledge the radical demographic shifts of this period.

A parallel story could be told on the other side of the Pennines, with the growth of the cotton spinning and weaving industry in Lancashire. Once again the Church of England responded, but all too slowly. Other parts of England – notably Staffordshire with its potteries – experienced a similar transformation in the late eighteenth and early nineteenth centuries; it was the beginning of what is now universally known as the industrial revolution. This series of changes was not, of course, the end of the story. The growth of industry and commerce presaged the slightly later expansive growth of new industrial towns, and eventually cities and conurbations. Parts of Lancashire and West Yorkshire are unusual in the concentration of urban growth in small and medium-sized towns, set within a surviving rural context. Nevertheless, great cities also grew – Manchester and Liverpool, Bradford and Leeds in this part of England. Most significantly of all, London grew to become the greatest city in the world, rising at its height to some eight million inhabitants. This growth came slightly after the growth of potteries and mills, with the expansion of vast Victorian housing developments from the 1850s onwards. Once again one can track the building of churches – sometimes, like St Bartholomew's at Armley in Leeds or St Augustine's, Kilburn in London, huge urban cathedrals. Other churches were more modest and less triumphalist. Still, however, church-building trailed seriously behind urban growth. Again there appeared to be an initial refusal to respond from the Church of England. Once it did respond it offered more pews than would ever have been needed.[1] Again, often Dissent was more effective in its early provision of places for worship, and notably in poorer areas.

The Church of England's slow response to the need to educate the urban poor showed a similar progression. Nonconformity moved more swiftly. The dissenting British and Foreign School Society, founded in 1807, preceded the foundation by the Church of England of the National Society, in 1811, which was established as a rival or competing body. These trends would eventually lead to latterly well-known outcomes. Nonconformity was the most effective engine of social reform, as far as the churches were concerned. So, for example, many of the early leaders of the Labour movement were nurtured in Methodist or other dissenting households.

Ironically, some of those who would have most influence in England from the Labour movement were from a Scottish Christian background, including Ramsay MacDonald and Keir Hardie. Hardie wrote: 'I claim for Socialism that it is the embodiment of Christianity in our industrial system,'[2] and then, far more bitingly, in his Christian message to the churches in 1897:

> When I think of the thousands of white-livered poltroons who will take the Christ's name in vain, and yet not see his image being crucified in every hungry child, I cannot think of peace . . . A holocaust of every church building in Christendom tonight would be an act of sweet savour in the sight of him whose name is supposed to be worshipped within their walls . . . We have no right to a merry Christmas, which so many of our fellows cannot share.[3]

So the energetic Labour Party was strengthened greatly by its religious roots; it was not, by and large, Marxist in its inspiration. Even into recent decades this legacy has survived. Len Murray, sometime general secretary of the TUC, was a Methodist; Tony Benn came from an independent Congregational family. Other notable examples could be multiplied. The point is, of course, that they were not sons of the established Church, the Church of England. Responding to these changes could hone or blunt the mission of all the Christian churches.

The effects of industrialization and urbanization on the Church's ability to care for and proclaim the gospel of peace and social justice to the English people can hardly be underestimated.

Building upon these reflections so far, then, this experience was to form the foundation upon which patterns of religious observance in the twentieth century would be based. Peter Berger has written: 'One of the most general characteristics of traditional pre-modern societies is their symbolic integration by means of religion. This integration is in most cases critically challenged by the onset of modernisation.'[4]

The precise effects of this process of modernization were twofold. The first of these we have just been alluding to, albeit implicitly: vast numbers of people moved from a largely agrarian life to an urban existence, engaged in the new and burgeoning industries which would cause Britain to be the richest and most powerful nation in the world for much of the Victorian age. The dissenting changes saw much more immediately the need to respond to these movements, both by building new churches and chapels, and through establishing new patterns of mission; the Methodist 'class system' was just one case in point. The Church of England was far slower to respond; we have commented already on apparent refusals. Even after the churches had made their respective shifts towards urban ministry, the coverage was often too sparse and too tardy or, ironically, later in the great cities too exaggerated. The movement away from patterns of rural life, with its dependence on, and closeness to, the natural order, and the vagaries of weather and harvests led to a breakdown in the earlier demographic patterns. New and very different urban communities began to be established. Pastoral care was patchy, and only intermittently effective. Living in urban areas contrasted sharply with earlier rural patterns. The parish system was simply replicated, as it had existed in the villages of pre-industrial England, and there was subsequently a failure to recognize and respond to these contrasts. It is easy to see how the new urban poor became lost to and ultimately alienated from the Church.

But the distancing of people from their dependence upon the elements and seasons has other, more profound, effects still upon patterns of piety and prayer. Throughout the working class it was not so much a drift into unbelief, free-thinking, agnosticism and otherwise. Instead, it was an unloosening of the immediate ties between prayer and the daily necessities of life. When families lived close to fields of corn, flocks of sheep or herds of cows, and the weather either threatened harvests or starved and burnt the grass on which cattle fed, the response was fairly clear. We should not be surprised that the 1662 Book of Common Prayer included prayers for 'rain, fair Weather and in time of Dearth and Famine'. There are some remarkable scenes in the film version of Thomas Hardy's novel *Far From the Madding Crowd* which press home this point with great vividness: the potentially devastating effects of an electric storm upon a harvest and upon harvested crops is one example; the fear issuing from a flock of sheep suffering from bloated stomachs makes the point in a different way – the shepherd pierces their stomachs to save their lives. In each case, both the livelihood of the farmer and his labourers, and also effects upon food supplies for the wider community are pressed home very sharply. Life was dependent upon the continuation of God's good providence

This movement, then, from the agrarian to the industrial, from the rural to the urban, had two separate, but interrelated, effects. We have already noted the different sorts of community which emerged from the shift from the land. Generally, even in small towns and urban villages, the communities were larger. The boundaries between local communities were blurred, and their daily and weekly rhythms less focused upon the church than had been the case within rural life. Ultimately, religion would become more marginal to daily life. In his magisterial analysis of secularization in the nineteenth century, Owen Chadwick writes:

> So the Industrial Revolution divided men from God . . . The statistic on which it rests is proven. Larger the town, smaller the percentage of persons who attended churches on Sundays . . . Whether or not decline in churchgoing is a sign of secularisation (and it probably is), bigger towns were a cause.[5]

Second, once the move had been made from a rural to an urban culture, so much of life became mediated rather than immediate.

Food was not grown locally for just one community; skills relating to daily life were not necessarily either needed or provided in one centre or within one village community; the production and processing of food and other daily necessities often now became, at least, one stage removed. Natural phenomena remained as significant as ever, but the effects were not experienced directly. Alongside the obvious changes effected by inadequate proclamation or pastoral care, these shifts also had an effect upon the nature of human reflection, and thus upon religious epistemology. In other words, these changes affected the way in which people came to *know* God, or indeed failed to do so. Mediated appreciation of natural phenomena will mean mediated knowing of God. What did – and indeed, does – this mean about the way Christians worship or do theology? At a more sophisticated level, this issue, among others, had clear effects upon the intellectual perception of Christianity. Critical historical study, biblical criticism and Darwin's theory of evolution all combined with these more basic, and almost subconscious, shifts to produce a Victorian crisis of faith which we shall explore a little later on.[6]

Signs of the effects spread more widely across Victorian society. So Owen Chadwick writes:

> The Victorian father goes to church. The Edwardian son stays at home. Is 'reason' the cause? Did reason prove or suggest that the activity was unprofitable, or meaningless, or even harmful? Did 'reason' suggest that the origins of religious awe lay in fear of earthquake or wind, uncontrollable terrors of nature and now that we are afraid no longer we can do without awe? After Durkheim, no-one who thought about the matter could answer these questions so easily or cheerfully.[7]

Durkheim dismissed this simplistic analysis, arguing that religious values were related to their ultimate social values. Society and religion, then, are inextricably linked. The literature of the time expressed this more vividly than any other source. Let that be the next tool in our analysis.

*

One of the most intriguing reflections upon this period was Edmund Gosse's retrospective biography of the relationship between himself and his father; Gosse's father was an eminent marine biologist and fundamentalist evangelical Christian.[8] Looking back on the purpose of this biographical memoir, Gosse wrote to Sydney Holland in January 1908:

> To tell the truth, what I should like to think my book to be – if the idea is not one of too great temerity – is a call to people to face the fact that the old faith is now impossible to sincere and intelligent minds, and that we must courageously face the difficulty of following entirely different ideals in moving forward towards the higher life. But what ideals, or (what is more important) what discipline can we substitute for the splendid metallic rigour of an earlier age?
>
> There must be found some guiding power, influencing artists, financiers, the meditative and imaginative, the self-centred, and the speculative alike.[9]

So what precisely does this say of shifts in belief in the Victorian age, particularly in the light of Edmund's father's, Philip Henry Gosse's, notable contribution to the advancement of science, and indeed his friendship with Charles Darwin? How did Henry Gosse square this circle? The short answer is that he did not do so, and this made his religious attitudes seem that much more bizarre. Edmund Gosse's critique of his father's religion is most famously portrayed in the story of the plum-pudding at Christmas time. Gosse wrote:

> On Christmas Day of this year 1857 our villa saw a very unusual sight. My father had given strictest charge that no difference whatever was to be made in our meals on that day; the dinner was to be neither more copious then usual, nor less so. He was obeyed, but the servants, secretly rebellious, made a small plum-pudding for themselves . . . Early in the afternoon, the maids . . . kindly remarked 'the poor dear child ought to have a bit, anyhow', and wheedled me into the kitchen, where I ate a slice of plum-pudding. Shortly I began to feel that pain inside, which, in my frail state, was inevitable, and my conscience smote me violently. At length I could bear my spiritual anguish no longer, and bursting into the study I called out: 'Oh! Papa, Papa, I

have eaten of flesh offered to idols!' It took some time between my sobs to explain what had happened. Then my father sternly said: 'Where is the accursed thing?' I explained that as much as was left of it was still on the kitchen table. He took me by the hand, and ran with me into the midst of the startled servants, seized what remained of the pudding ... flung the idolatrous confectionery on to the middle of the ashes, and then raked it deep down into the mass.[10]

This is a remarkable tale by any standards, and through it Edmund Gosse illustrates with great power the chasm that was to open up between him and his father on the matter of religion. Whether this incident ever occurred, however, may be a moot point. In her excellent, illuminating and revisionist biography of the father, Philip Henry Gosse, Ann Thwaite makes clear the tendentious nature of much of the account of the family relationships in *Father and Son*. Careful reading of correspondence between Edmund and Henry Gosse makes clear both the bonds of affection and the exaggerated nature of Edmund's account.[11] Nevertheless, the very exaggeration itself indicates the distance which Edmund had moved from belief. There is no doubting the fundamentalist nature of Henry Gosse's Christian faith, but his son's own alienation from it leads to further exaggeration. Here is but one extreme example of how the emerging culture could find itself in conflict with certain evangelical versions of the Christian gospel. Admittedly Gosse was an 'extreme' independent Protestant Christian and hardly mainstream, but his was one reaction to an apparently faithless world. In Edmund, too, there is a clear reaction to it. How effective were the churches in living and teaching the Christian gospel in this changing climate?

Other novelists imply, or hint at, a lack of charity or empathy within much Christian teaching. Charles Dickens did not embrace the Christian faith very formally, and his social criticism often hints at a church and an establishment which was less than sympathetic to the needs of the time. One particularly touching episode in *Bleak House* captures this feeling precisely. *Bleak House* is Dickens' most wide-ranging and symbolic novel, and throughout there is an underlying compassion which borders on sentimentality. Among the most pathetic characters in the novel is Little Jo, who eventually dies of disease and malnutrition; most revealing of Dickens' religious instincts is the scene where Jo is dying. Allan Woodcourt, one of the heroes of the novel, asks:

'Jo! Did you ever know a prayer?'
'Never knowd nothink, sir.'
'Not so much as one short prayer?'
'No, sir. Nothink at all. Mr Chadbands he was a-prayin wunst at Mr Sangsby's and I heerd him, but he sounded as if he was a-speaking to hisself, and not to me. He prayed a lot, but *I* couldn't make out nothink on it.'

There is no cynicism in this passage. The stricken young man asks to go to the burial ground – somewhere he has haunted throughout his tragically short life. The lad continues:

'It's turned very dark, sir. Is there any light a-coming?'
'It's coming fast, Jo. Jo, can you say what I say?'
'I'll say anythink as you say, sir, for I knows it's good.'

Struggling in his dying weakness, the boy is taught by Woodcourt:

'OUR FATHER.'
'Our Father! – yes, that's very good, sir.'
'WHICH ART IN HEAVEN.'
'Art in Heaven – is the light a-comin, sir?'
'It is close at hand. HALLOWED BE THY NAME!'
'Hallowed be-thy-'

The light is come upon the dark benighted way.[12]

The child is dead.

The whole novel is suffused with a feeling of charity and compassion which again and again echoes instincts at the heart of the Christian gospel. Compassion is rooted in a generosity that issues from human nature at its best. The religion depicted by Dickens, then, is a form of natural religion or religiosity, and not that purveyed by the churches, or certainly not, as he sees it, by the established Church of England. Indeed, the novel has a strong feeling of social critique, much of which is aimed at the establishment. The legal profession receives the most explicit and excoriating swipes from Dickens' pen, but the hierarchical nature of society and those institutions which support this are implicitly criticized too.

This indicates, as hinted at both in Owen Chadwick and thus earlier in Durkheim's reflections, that movements within Victorian society were complex, and that the shifts were not simply related to an inability to believe.[13] This is most markedly clear in the work of Thomas Hardy and in his own experience of Victorian society, which led him to write as he did. Indeed, A. N. Wilson comments:

> Hardy is certainly the most religious of all great English novelists, the most spiritually engaged of all great Victorian writers. He went on regarding himself, after a fashion, as a churchman. He went on hoping all his days for intellectual candour from the Church, and was bitterly disappointed by its failure to speak seriously to modern thinking minds.[14]

Hardy's own copy of the Authorized Version of the Bible was annotated in extraordinary detail. His novels and poetry bear witness to his knowledge of both Holy Scripture and the life of the Church of England. *Jude the Obscure*, his last novel, is coloured by much autobiographical influence as it moves from Jude's clear sense of having a vocation to the ordained ministry, to his drift into agnosticism and free-thinking as his relationship with Sue Bridehead deepens. Hardy's movement away from Christian orthodoxy was, however, as much affected by sociological factors as by theological. The son of a journeyman builder, he could never forget his humble social roots. Attitudes within the nineteenth-century Church of England seemed to reinforce the snobbishness of Victorian society and the Church's lack of empathy with working people, notably, in this case, in Hardy's home area of Wessex.[15]

It is brought out sharply again and again, but perhaps nowhere so poignantly as in *Tess of the D'Urbervilles*. Tess approaches the vicar of her own village, Marlott, asking that her dying illegitimate child (by Alec D'Urberville) be baptized before the child dies. The request is refused. Later she encounters the cold Calvinism of James Clare, the vicar of Emminster and father of her lover, Angel. The blend of harsh, uncompromising theology with social condescension is very effectively portrayed in these pages. Despite all this, however, as A. N. Wilson hints, Hardy never entirely gives up on the Christian religion. In the preface to his late (1922) collection of poems, *Late Lyrics and Earlier*, he writes:

the historic and once august hierarchy of Rome some generations ago lost its chance of being the religion of the future by . . . throwing over the little band of New Catholics who were making a struggle for continuity by applying the principle of evolution to their own faith, joining hands with modern science, and outflanking the hesitating English instinct towards liturgical restatement (a flank march which at the time I quite prepared to witness, with the gathering of many millions into its fold).[16]

The reference here is to the 'Catholic Modernists' suppressed by the Vatican in the early years of the twentieth century. Hardy goes on to reflect:

It may indeed be a forlorn hope, a mere dream, that of an alliance between religion, which must be retained unless the world is to perish, and complete rationality, which must come, unless also the world is to perish, by means of the interfusing effect of poetry.[17]

This, then, is a rather more sanguine view of the Christian religion than that of Edmund Gosse. Other writers, notably George Eliot in *Silas Marner*, also sought for an empathy within Victorian society, which they believed religion had lost. Anthony Trollope used satire to express his own unhappiness with the established Church, and to point up his increasing scepticism. That patterns of religious observance were changing is demonstrated through a reference in a rather different sort of literature, notably Flora Thompson's portrait of rural Oxfordshire in the 1880s and 1890s. She notes, for example:

If the Lark Rise people had been asked their religion, the answer of nine out of ten would have been 'Church of England', for practically all of them were christened, married and buried as such, although in adult life, few went to church between the baptisms of their offspring. The children were shepherded there after Sunday School and about a dozen of their elders attended regularly.[18]

Each of these writers reflects different aspects of a disillusionment with Christianity and the churches during the nineteenth century. Even so, it would be facile to suggest that the churches did not try to respond to the changing cultural and demographic climate. Some would argue that these responses were themselves so inappropriate or misdirected as to increase the alienation of many from the Christian faith. Can that opinion be allowed to stand? Ought Edmund Gosse to be allowed to have the last word?

*

Such a rhetorical question implies an obvious tendentiousness. Certainly, to vindicate Gosse would be to read his biographical reflections in a manner that Ann Thwaite's scholarship will not allow. Attempts to respond effectively to a changing culture go much further back, to the eighteenth century and to the Enlightenment. Some of the most interesting and radical responses issued from Germany. Before 1800, both Lessing and Reimarus had asked fiercely critical questions about the Bible and its witness. After 1800, the critical study of Scripture continued relentlessly. Sometimes, as in the case of David Friedrich Strauss' *Life of Jesus*, the result would be the opposite of apologetics; instead of building up faith, the questions raised led towards agnosticism. Interestingly enough, it would be George Eliot, the novelist, who would translate Strauss' work into English; she too became a free-thinker. Elsewhere the work of theologians would bear more positive fruit for the churches, and for an apologetic approach to the Christian gospel. Perhaps the classical example of early liberalism is the work of F. D. E. Schleiermacher. His *Religion: Speeches to its Cultured Despisers* sought to do precisely what its title implies. His later, constructive work – in its English translation titled simply *The Christian Faith* – approached faith from the starting point of religious experience and religious 'self-consciousness'. Such self-consciousness, he argued, was a quality which exists in all of us to a greater or lesser degree.

Alongside this scholarly response, and sometimes integrated with it, there arose a series of different 'religious' responses and revivals. We have already encountered Wesley, Whitefield and the different branches of early Methodism, and the Church of England's failure to embrace these movements within its own heart. Wesley's itinerant ministry, and his engagement with the emergent new urban poor, was to leave a legacy already adverted to in the growth of the labour movement towards the end of the nineteenth century. Already by then, however, Methodism and other dissenting groups were beginning to become gentrified and to drift in an increasingly middle-class direction. Nevertheless, there is no doubting the impact that Methodism had within the new, and growing, urban areas. This was also true to some extent of some other branches of Dissent. It was undeniably true of that other growing 'nonconformist' minority, the increasing Roman Catholic population within England. Devastating poverty, allied to the tragedy of the Potato Famine in the 1840s, led to increasing immigration from Ireland into England. That meant that the Roman Catholic Church was dealing with proportionately more poor people. So, undoubtedly, it was the Roman Catholic Church, emancipated by the Parliamentary Act of 1829, and encouraged by the re-establishment of an English hierarchy in 1850 under the leadership of Cardinal Wiseman, which was most effective among all the churches in ministering to the urban poor. Even so, this remained a ministry almost entirely to a minority sub-culture, and, in general it had little impact upon the wider population. There were exceptions to this, as we shall see towards the end of this chapter.

What of revival within the Church of England itself? There is a sense in which all the way through, from the seventeenth century onwards, there were groups within the established Church committed to different ways of recovering what they believed to be a true understanding of the nature of the Church, an understanding which would make the Church faithful and effective in its ministry to the people of England. It was, indeed, for these reasons that even earlier on, during the Elizabethan period, Richard Hooker had written his *Laws of Ecclesiastical Polity*, charting a careful course between Counter-Reformation *Roman* Catholicism (as it is now labelled) and the extremes of the Anabaptists and Calvinist Puritan churchmen. At the end of the seventeenth century, the 'non-juring' bishops who were deposed from their sees following the accession to the throne of William III represented one strand within that broader group, often referred to as 'High Church Tories'. This continuing tendency within the Church of England represented those who were keen to retain an emphasis on the historical continuity of the Catholic Church within the Church of England. Such views were held by the so-called 'Caroline Divines' during the Laudian period in the early seventeenth century, including Bishop Lancelot Andrewes among their number. This inheritance remained as a significant tendency within the eighteenth century, with writers like Daniel Waterland and Charles Wheatly. It was also the High Churchmen who were eventually responsible (through the Scottish Episcopal Succession) for the possibility of Samuel Seabury being consecrated bishop for Anglicans in the newly independent United States of America.

Towards the end of the eighteenth century, however, in the wake of the birth of Methodism, other groups began to exert an important influence. Notably there was that coterie of evangelicals, grouped around John Venn, the rector of Clapham from 1792 to 1813. Popularly known as the Clapham Sect and including Zachary Macaulay, Henry Thornton and William Wilberforce, these pious and politically conservative churchmen were nevertheless committed to good works. Thomas Clarkson, who as it happened never lived in Clapham, was the untiring traveller and collector of evidence who abandoned his clerical career, remaining a deacon, to engage in the crusade against slavery in the British Empire. He worked hand in glove with the Clapham Sect. His extraordinary commitment, and the tenacity of the entire group in working to dismantle the structures of slavery, was typical of this earthed evangelical fervour which manifested itself in good works.

They worked tirelessly, not only for the abolition of the slave trade but also for the extension of Sunday Schools and for general moral improvement in England. They also comprised the key people who established the British and Foreign Bible Society. Hence, despite their conservative political starting point, here was a committed group who could see the need for new initiatives in order that the Church might respond to an increasingly complex social order. At about the same time another group of High Churchmen paralleled the Clapham Sect. Focused on the work of Joshua Watson, they took their name from the place where Watson's brother was rector in east London; they became known as the Hackney Phalanx. Joshua Watson mirrored the Clapham Sect's commitment to foreign mission and also to the advancement of education in England. He was a classical High Church Tory, not wedded to an Erastian view of Church and state, but nevertheless keen on the Establishment. Again, then, the base was politically conservative, but expended much effort and money on 'good causes'. In both these groups the gospel was seen to have social implications, even if these implications did not include a radical reform of the social order, except, of course, in the case of the international slave trade. Certainly, they saw the need for the Church to gird its loins and to minister more effectively to the rapidly increasing population of urban England, the key issue with which this chapter began; indeed, this group was partly responsible for early attempts to build more churches in the newly burgeoning urban areas.

The work of the Clapham Sect formed the foundation for a wider evangelical revival, and a succession of remarkable leaders, including Henry Venn, Charles Simeon, Henry Martin and others, was to exert an influence which continues still. There were several links across to the Calvinistic Methodism of George Whitefield and his supporters. As well as pressing for a more effective and biblically based ministry, there was also a commitment to social issues. The seventh Lord Shaftesbury, a notable evangelical, initiated the Factory Acts. He was also responsible for pressing the cause of removing women and children from working in the mines and collieries, and indeed for pushing forward the Climbing Chimney Boys Act, which forbade the use of young boys in chimney-sweeping, as campaigned against by Charles Kingsley and other early Christian Socialists.

Among those to be influenced profoundly by the evangelical revival was John Henry Newman (1801–90). Newman went on to be ordained to the evangelical parish of St Clement in Oxford, but during his time there his friendship began to grow with John Keble and Edward Bouverie Pusey in an attempt to recover what they believed to be a 'purer' and more patristically based understanding of the Church. This alliance would ultimately lead to the birth of the Tractarian or Oxford Movement, which, again, was concerned to respond to the changing social and intellectual conditions of the times.

The Oxford Movement brought together an interesting and varied collection of strands. Effectively, its beginning is marked by John Keble preaching the Assize Sermon in 1833 at St Mary's Church in Oxford, under the title of 'National Apostasy'. In his sermon, Keble denounced the action of the government in suppressing a number of Irish bishoprics. In retrospect the cause seems obscure, even bizarre. The Church of Ireland, established as it was, represented a tiny minority of the people of Ireland. Against this canvas it had inherited far too many episcopal sees in relation to its contemporary needs. For this reason the government's action was understandable. Keble's point, however, was not related to the logic of the government's action. Instead it was an attack on Erastianism: that is, on too close a connection between Church and state. It was more than inappropriate, he argued, for the government to take such action in matters ecclesiastical. The gospel is there to be a counter to assumed human values. Edward Bouverie Pusey had a rather different pedigree. He had started out as a biblical scholar, strongly influenced by the advance of critical scholarship in Germany; he was, then, for that time, a fairly rare example of an English critical biblical scholar. As the Oxford Movement found its feet, however, Pusey left such scholarship behind and devoted himself to a more 'conservative' striving for continuity with the ancient Patristic tradition, influenced by the writings of John Henry Newman.

Newman was undoubtedly the greatest intellect of the Oxford Movement, and it was largely his work that would lead to this group becoming known as the Tractarians. He and others were responsible for writing a series of 'tracts' aimed at setting out principles for re-establishing the catholicity of the Church of England, and thus its part within the wider 'Great Church'. Tract XC, published in 1841, argued that the Thirty-nine Articles, one of the Reformation period foundation documents or 'formularies' of the Church of England, condemned none of the catholic beliefs and practices which it was assumed that it was originally written to condemn. Tract XC received a very hostile press and, in the wake of this, Newman resigned the living of St Mary's Oxford to live a semi-monastic life at Littlemore, on the outskirts of the city. Pursuing the inexorable logic which now directed him, he sought to prove that the Roman Catholic Church – to which he was increasingly attracted – was indeed the true and undoubted successor of the infant Church of the Patristic period. This was argued extensively in his *Essay on the Development of Christian Doctrine*.[19]

Ironically, the conservative aims of his research would effectively produce what might now be considered to be one of the most radical theological theses propounded by an English writer in the nineteenth century. For the method Newman chose to 'prove' continuity of the Church over the centuries was to postulate a process of *development*. In other words, the form of the Church, as it was received in his time, was a development of the Church as it had been in the early period; this principle could be applied, then, to the whole of the deposit of Christian doctrine. The radical implications are fairly obvious. If doctrine has so developed, then it can develop further. Furthermore, if doctrine can develop, then how does one decide which is a proper development and which is, so to speak, a rogue growth? Newman hedged his thesis round with clear 'tests' to attempt to forestall such difficulties.

Nonetheless, the significance of Newman's thesis was crucial in the movement of theological ideas in the eighteenth and nineteenth centuries.[20]

Looking at his essay now, it is difficult to sustain his argument as it is set out in the 'tests'. The notion, for example, that doctrine unfolds like a flower, (which is at the heart of Newman's thesis), and that everything that is later manifested is effectively there from the start, proved both too little and too much. It proved too little in trying to safeguard an unchanging body of dogma which, nevertheless, undeniably has developed; can this really be sustained? It seems unlikely, since the same argument collapses into the danger of the theory proving too much. If all that is there now was there, latently, from the beginning, then how much more might still arise, and where might it take us? Have we not in fact stumbled upon an incipient theory of doctrinal evolution?[21] For many now, these questions are invigorating rather than frightening; they may also explain why attempts within the Roman Catholic Church to canonize Newman have moved so very slowly. He is seen by some as an incipient radical and a potential relativizer. The issues which he pinpoints do, of course, raise interesting parallels in nineteenth-century thought more generally, and, indeed, most obviously, with the work of Charles Darwin on evolution. It seems likely that the train of thought initiated by Newman stands alongside other cultural shifts represented by elements of developmental and evolutionary thought within science, theology and politics during the Victorian period. From another point of view, more positively it can be seen as the Church trying to react to the call crystallized in those lines quoted earlier from Thomas Hardy, where he would plead for the Church to respond to changing patterns of thought and culture.[22]

The Oxford Movement continued to flourish, even after Newman's secession to the Roman Catholic Church in 1845. Indeed, it broadened out to embrace both ritualistic and social teachings and trends. The ritualistic movement had its moments of crisis in battles with Lord Shaftesbury in the 1860s, and in the trial of Bishop Edward King of Lincoln in the very first years of the twentieth century. Nonetheless, ultimately ritualism would introduce more colour to a far wider spectrum of the Church of England than simply to its Anglo-Catholic wing; even surpliced choirs were an early fruit of the movement! Socially, Anglo-Catholicism has left a rich inheritance, and early on this shift was closely associated with ritualist developments. So, for example, Fathers Lowder and Wainwright, at St Peter's, London Docks, exemplified the Tractarian emphasis on both ritualism and a committed ministry to the poor. In the 1870s, Lowder reflected: 'There was a large number of small trades people, costermongers, persons engaged about the docks, lightermen, watermen coal-whippers . . . the poorer of whom . . . were . . . unable to support their families.'[23] Lowder, Wainwright and others like them were convicted by the gospel to minister to them in their hardship. It is, of course, easy both to romanticize such ministries and to claim too much for their influence. Certainly, this ministry remained largely paternalistic in its approach, not least because of the narrowness of the recruitment of clergy to the Church of England in the nineteenth century; most were drawn from the upper-middle and land-owning classes.[24] Even so, some of the explicit and implicit criticisms levelled by Charles Dickens, George Eliot and Thomas Hardy were being addressed.

The Roman Catholic Church too began to increase its effectiveness beyond the limits of a confined sub-culture. This was most dramatically demonstrated by Henry Edward Manning, a former Anglican archdeacon and later Cardinal Archbishop of Westminster, who intervened very effectively in the London Dock strike of 1889. Manning, again from an upper-middle-class background, developed a social radicalism which issued from an understanding of the terrifying social inequities of late Victorian

England. Manning was instrumental in getting the striking dockers their sixpence an hour, and his own physical image was later even woven into a local trade union banner. Such had been the effect of his intervention that his funeral brought out on to the streets of London people from every background and class. A. N. Wilson describes the scene lyrically:

> Many Londoners had never seen such a sight – hundreds of priests, monks and friars in their mediaeval habits, singing their solemn Gregorian chant set out in procession to Kensal Green cemetery ... But these enchantments of the Middle Ages were accompanied by figures quite new in history: behind the Funeral Car were the National League, United Kingdom Alliance, Trades Unions of London, Dockers' Societies, Amalgamated Society of Stevedores, Federation of Trades and Labour Unions, Independent Order of Coal Templars and Universal Mercy Board Movement ... And for every step of that four-mile journey, the pavements were thickly lined with crowds. At some points, they were so dense that the procession was halted.[25]

Wilson describes here an extraordinary scene, and one which shows the Church *in* England having touched the hearts of great numbers of people. Furthermore, those hearts which had been touched were not only those of the great and the good; most of those people in the crowds on the road from Brompton Oratory to Kensal Green were ordinary Londoners, many of them, perhaps, from working-class communities. This was a telling moment, and indicated that the churches could still touch the hearts of a wide range of people across English society. But could such moves proliferate?

It is often said that the failure of the churches in England, within the nineteenth century, was once more a case of 'too little, too late'. It may be that the Church of England is particularly vulnerable to this criticism, although retrospective wisdom is generally easier than knowing how best to respond at the time. Even this survey, however, has highlighted the complexity of the background and the enormous cultural shifts of the period. The churches did try to respond, and sometimes heroically. Nevertheless, as earlier chapters have indicated, the uncertainties of the relationship between the Church *in* England, and the people of England, reach back well beyond Victorian times. Cultural change, in its widest sense, extends right back to the period of the English reformations. There is no doubt about the missed opportunities of the churches over a period of almost five centuries. Equally, there is no doubt of the difficulties posed by the shifting ground on which the churches have found themselves standing. In which direction have things gone in the twentieth century, and, moreover, what has happened in the New World?

5

Never such innocence again

———•◦•———

Never such innocence,
Never before or since,
As changed itself to past
Without a word – the men
Leaving the gardens tidy,
The thousands of marriages
Lasting a little while longer:
Never such innocence again.[1]

The twentieth century could easily be dubbed 'the age of lost innocence'. Philip Larkin's sharp and evocative poem describes an 'existential' loss of innocence following the meaningless carnage of the Great War. But in different ways, as the century unfolded, so one innocence after another appeared to fold before the pressures of cultural change. How did this affect religion and the churches? Were the hearts of the English people touched either positively or negatively by these profound shifts within British society and culture? Larkin's reflections are not posed at a highbrow level; instead they are about ordinary people and the effects of the 1914–18 war upon them. The poem is titled 'MCMXIV' and its first stanza runs:

Those long uneven lines
Standing as patiently
As if they were stretched outside
The Oval or Villa Park.
The crowns of hats, the sun
On moustached archaic faces
Grinning as if it were all
An August Bank Holiday lark;

So Larkin's lines reflect his take on the people of England as their collective subconscious passed through the searing lens of the terrible conflict which encompassed so much of the so-called civilized world. The effects of the Great War upon European civilization are now widely recognized and many see 1914 as the end of the Victorian era and the beginning of modern culture. One recent review of the period talks of 1914–1991 as the short twentieth century.[2] Undoubtedly it was the Great War that wrought the most far-reaching and profound changes, not only upon English culture but upon human self-understanding across the world. Was the First World War the cultural earthquake that ushered in what we now describe as globalization? Certainly, from now on, it is impossible to view English religion as a uniquely English phenomenon. The hearts of the English people would hereafter be touched by shock waves of a global nature too.

Interestingly enough, this was true even before the outbreak of war, with regard to theology and the Christian Church. Other seismic changes had already been occurring around the turn of the century and, most notably, with the flowering of the Modernist movement within Roman Catholicism. This was by no means a purely English phenomenon either. Indeed, one might see the key epicentre as France. Nevertheless, it spilled out across Europe, and England was another source of tremors, with the work of George Tyrrell, Alfred Lilley and Baron Friedrich von Hügel. Hints of the significance of this group of theologians were picked up by the novelist Thomas Hardy; we saw a reference to this in the previous chapter. This is interesting in itself inasmuch as the Modernist movement and the crisis it provoked might best be seen as the final impact of movements in nineteenth-century thought. Returning to the theme of a loss of innocence, Catholic Modernism might well be labelled as the key indicator of this within Christian thought – never such theological innocence again.

Catholic Modernism as a phenomenon should be set within the context of the great shifts which had followed the Enlightenment and the growth of modern experimental science. Darwin's work on evolution stood alongside other patterns of developmental thinking. Within the theological community John Henry Newman is undoubtedly the seminal figure in England, and in his later life within Roman Catholicism. It is interesting to reflect upon Newman's work and its impact upon Roman Catholic thought. Some Catholics would still see the publication of his *Essay on the Development of the Christian Doctrine*[3] as the first step on the slippery slope towards 'indifferentism' and relativism. Although Newman hedged his theory around with a series of 'tests' which would protect Christian theology and the churches from unacceptable developments, nonetheless his writing still heralded an approach that postulated a continuing process of development since the apostolic and sub-apostolic period. Interestingly enough, his former Anglican co-worker and fellow Tractarian, Edward Bouverie Pusey, had in his early period of scholarship been influenced by new work in German biblical studies. This work, and the emergence later in the nineteenth century of Adolf von Harnack and the Liberal Protestant school, paralleled the rise of Catholic Modernism in the final decade of the nineteenth century and the first decade of the twentieth.

What, then, were the roots and the character of Catholic Modernism and what were its effects? First of all it would be misleading to see Catholic Modernism as a unified movement. It was instead a series of attempts, sometimes in conflict with each other, to relate Roman Catholic dogma to the modern world. Second, it would be wrong to see modernism as being parallel with, and in concert with, the aims and methods of Liberal Protestantism. Indeed, in certain cases it aimed deliberately to criticize that movement and to offer a 'yet more excellent way'. This is seen most clearly in the trenchant writings of one of the most important of the English Modernists, George Tyrrell. Indeed, often he writes vehemently and polemically. So:

> They [the Liberal Protestants] wanted to bring Jesus into the nineteenth century as the Incarnation of its ideal of the Divine Righteousness, i.e. of all the highest principles and aspirations that ensure the healthy progress of civilisation ... With eyes thus preoccupied they could only find the German in the Jew; a moralist in a visionary; a professor in a prophet; the nineteenth century in the first; the natural in the supernatural.[4]

It was Albert Schweitzer's *The Quest for the Historical Jesus* that was seen by many as the conclusion and the death knell of both Liberal Protestantism and the nineteenth-century quest for the historical Jesus. Schweitzer had seen Jesus' ministry as

apocalyptic and eschatological – ushering in a new age. Tyrrell
had effectively accepted Schweitzer's eschatological conclusions
and this made his criticism of the Liberal Protestant enterprise
that much sharper. His most famous critical aphorism ran:
'The Christ that Harnack sees, looking back through nineteen
centuries of Catholic darkness, is only the reflection of a Liberal
Protestant face, seen at the bottom of a deep well.'[5]

So, parallel though these movements may have been, their aims
were not consistent. Instead, Tyrrell, for example, was keen to
show how the *idea* (using this in the same sense as Newman) of
the Christ of eschatology – as authorized by Schweitzer – was to
prepare and hasten the kingdom. Hence the mysterious, transcendent Christ was embodied in Catholicism and so there was
no chasm between the gospel and the Church. Even this single
reflection on Tyrrell makes it clear that one of the 'crimes' for
which modernism was finally indicted by the Vatican – that is
too great a stress on immanence – is precisely the opposite of
that which Tyrrell aims to prove. Tyrrell was keen to keep together the transcendent Christ of faith with the 'Jesus of history'
whom the Liberal Protestants had sought so hard to recover.
It was the separation of these two by the German Protestant
scholars which Tyrrell aimed to counter. He wrote: 'If Christ
spoke and had to speak the language of pure transcendence, His
whole life and teaching and spirit implied the truth of immanence.'[6] And later he adds:

> Through the mystical body, animated by the Spirit, we are
> brought into immediate contact with the ever present
> Christ. We hear Him in its Gospel, we touch and handle
> Him in its sacraments. He lives on in the Church, not
> metaphorically, but actually.[7]

This excursion into the thought of George Tyrrell gives a snapshot of just one modernist. Similar snapshots of others, both in
England and elsewhere in Europe, also very swiftly indicate the
breadth and variety in the 'movement'. Rather than a movement
there were a number of scholars with no common programme,
working in different countries and differing widely among themselves. So there was a social modernism in France comprising
Christian democrats; there was the biblical critical strand in
Alfred Loisy; in Tyrrell we have seen a dogmatic strand; Maurice

Blondel was a 'philosopher of action'; Friedrich von Hügel was a mystic. If there was a common strand it was to bring Catholic belief into closer relationship with contemporary culture and philosophy. The social element within all this indicates that there was a clear practical outflow; the philosophical/theological element points to the aim of a proper apologetic. Alec Vidler writes that commonly they had 'a desire in one way or another to promote the adaptation of Catholicism, of the Church and its teaching, to new conditions'.[8]

This desire too (and we have seen this already in Tyrrell) was to be pursued from within the Catholic Church. It was not an individualistic or an independent scholarship pursued purely within the academy. The scholars saw themselves as church theologians. Hence, when Loisy fell foul of the authorities and eventually in 1906 abandoned his Christian priestly work, it was an enormous blow to him. Vidler again writes:

> The English tend to suppose that anyone who wishes to do so is entitled to call himself a Christian without regard to membership of a church. This subjective and individualistic attitude had never seemed reasonable to Loisy. He took it for granted that to be a Christian meant to be a member of a church, and it was for the Church to say who were and who were not its members. An individual professing to be a Christian without being a member of a church was a contradiction in terms.[9]

This attitude, manifested by so many – if not all – of the Catholic Modernists, is directly germane to our theme. In other words, how has the Church (and more specifically the Church in England) related to the hearts of the people? The story of Catholic Modernism is one of an unfolding of a great tragedy, which affected not only individual lives but also the effectiveness of the Christian Church more widely to proclaim the faith credibly and intelligently in quite new circumstances. Within the pontificate of Pope Leo XIII, Modernism was tolerated, but with the accession of his successor, Pius X, the climate changed radically. With the encouragement of his Secretary of State, Cardinal Merry del Val, he rounded on the Modernists. The decree *Lamentibili sane exitu* was issued in July 1907 and, together with the September 1907 encyclical, *Pascendi dominici gregis*, it condemned Modernism. Through the motu proprio *Sacrorum antistitum* this policy was put fully into effect. All clergy were required at their ordination to take the Anti-Modernist oath, and this requirement remained in force all the way through the twentieth century up until after the Vatican II reforms.

The effect of this on individuals was devastating. We have already encountered Loisy's response and demise with regard to the Church. Tyrrell, however, exemplifies the tragedy more sharply perhaps than anyone else. He was expelled from the Jesuits and, through his marginalization from the Church, he gradually moved further from Catholic orthodoxy. He died, given the last rites of the Church, but was refused a Catholic burial and was indeed buried in the Anglican churchyard in Storrington, where his friend and literary executor, Maud Petre, was eventually buried alongside him. Similar tales of persecution and marginalization followed with others like Henri Brémond. What precisely then was the charge placed against the modernists, and what was the lasting effect? Gabriel Daly quotes Ludwig Ott as summarizing perfectly the teaching of *Pascendi*:

> The cognitional theoretical basis of Modernism, is agnosticism, according to which human rational cognition is limited to the world of experience. Religion, according to this theory, develops from the principle of vital immanence (immanentism), that is, from the need for God, which dwells in the human soul. The truths of religion are, according to the general progress of culture, caught up in a constant substantial development (evolutionism).[10]

Putting aside the jargon, the accusation is fairly clear. Modernism compromises the tradition and capitulates to Enlightenment rationalism. But even the brief extract from Tyrrell, quoted earlier, gives lie to this. Further on in the introduction to his book, Gabriel Daly notes: 'It is high time for Roman Catholic theologians to cease making ritual obeisances towards the myth of a concerted modernist threat to the unity, orthodoxy and stability of the Church.'[11]

And, later, towards the end of his conclusion Daly writes:

> Credible Christian theology can no longer take its stand upon a rigid dichotomy between transcendence and

immanence. Events, however, have committed it to a search for transcendence within total human experience just at the moment when that experience is revealing further, unsuspecting and bewildering depths.[12]

Catholic Modernism's defeat, then, in the first years of the twentieth century undoubtedly left its scars. Daly has hinted at its effects upon the Roman Catholic Church itself. *Pascendi*'s response to modernism effectively made all Roman Catholic theology for the next half-century reactive to a particular parodied, and hopelessly over-systematized caricature of the writings of a very varied group of modernist writers. Of *Pascendi* Daly writes: 'it can be read with compelling interest, not so much for what it says about the modernists, as for its effect upon the following half-century of Roman Catholic theology.'[13]

Thomas Hardy alluded to the efforts of this condemnation on the way in which wider culture responded to the Christian faith during that period. At a time when anti-clericalism was beginning to bite in the academic world, the effects of *Pascendi* and the associated documents would send out shock waves well beyond the formal bounds of the Church. Since it would affect every ordained priest in the Roman Catholic Church, and their ministry would be broad, it was not just 'high culture' that would be affected. Furthermore, modernism was respected beyond the Roman Communion. Alec Vidler, one of the most well-read scholars of Catholic Modernism, was himself something of an Anglican example of that breed. His comments on Loisy's embracing of the Church make it clear that he too saw that an open and critical approach to the tradition should still rest within the Church. The further implication is that the Church would be that much more effective if it engaged more subtly with culture. The defeat of Catholic Modernism and the mode of that defeat was undoubtedly a dire 'missed opportunity'. Such defeat, however, could not bury the theological insights gained, and as the Great War loomed nearer there could certainly be 'never such theological innocence again'. Even the retrenching which came with Karl Barth during that war could not unsay what had been said.

*

If one ever had doubts of the effects of the Great War on human culture and civilization, just a brief glance at the poetry which issued from it should be sufficient to change one's mind. Even those writers often seen as more reticent find themselves changed by the horror and apparent meaninglessness of the conflict. Thomas Hardy, unquestionably a nineteenth-century figure, finds his poetry changed by the conflict. So, 'In Time of "The Breaking of Nations"':

> Only a man harrowing clods
>   In a slow silent walk
> With an old horse that stumbles and nods
>   Half asleep as they stalk.
>
> Only thin smoke without flame
>   From heaps of couch-grass;
> Yet this will go on the same
>   Though dynasties pass.[14]

Rudyard Kipling, apparently fashioned by imperialism and the 'white man's burden', has his consciousness tortured and scarred through the loss of his son:

> If any question why we died,
> Tell them, because our fathers lied.[15]

He saw through the smoke of battle to the loss of innocence. Religious images are pressed into service:

> The Garden called Gethsemane,
>   It held a pretty lass,
> But all the time she talked to me
>   I prayed my cup might pass . . .
> It didn't pass, it didn't pass
>   It didn't pass from me.
> I drank it when we met the gas
>   Beyond Gethsemane.[16]

Both of these writers had their consciousness transformed without even being near the lines. The effect on Wilfred Owen, Siegfried Sassoon, Robert Graves, Edmund Blunden and so many others is counted not only in the poetry that issued from them, but also in the memoirs which attempted to describe and pass a critical yet merciful eye over the carnage. In more recent years that most perceptive piece of social criticism, the *Blackadder* television series, perhaps acted as the sharpest commentary of all on the First World War. The humour is couched cynically, and in the final episode the sense of tragedy is not even disguised. The entire cast go over the top to their death. One of the key elements, uncovered again through television, is the way in which the military campaign both emphasized and, at the same time, obliterated class divisions. The division into privates, non-commissioned and commissioned officers perpetuated the class consciousness which already bedevilled English society. Nevertheless, the exigencies of life in the trenches and the basic and appalling conditions meant that all were in it together. *Blackadder,* through the medium of television, focuses this poignantly with humour. Novelists too have queried this vein effectively. Susan Hill's *Strange Meeting* explores a profound relationship which grows up in the trenches between two men of very different 'social station'. So, although to all intents and purposes the old order continues, in fact the sheer extremities of human experience mean that the living out of this old order in such close conditions is itself the dynamic catalyst of change. The fixed order of society proves itself meaningless. Some of Hardy's poetry at the outset of the war assumes that the world is still as it has been, even though Hardy himself is arguably the greatest novelist of the agrarian revolution of the nineteenth century. Although there are certainly hints of profound change in 'Men Who March Away':

> Hence the faith and fire within us
> > Men who march away
> > Ere the barn-cocks say
> > Night is growing grey;
> Leaving all that here can win us;
> Hence the faith and fire within us
> > Men who march away.[17]

Hardy had a good sense of history, and that too would take a knock within this most unreasonable of all conflicts. Paul Fussell writes perceptively:

> Furthermore, the Great War was perhaps the last to be conceived as taking place within a seamless, purposeful 'history' involving a coherent stream of time running from past through present to future.

and so he notes a little later:

the Great War took place in what was, compared with ours, a static world, where the values appeared stable and where the meanings of abstractions seemed permanent and reliable.[18]

These shifts, then, which questioned the ordering of society and the meaning of history would create a new consciousness, and not just in the 'chattering classes' and the world of intellectual reflection. It would permeate every element and sub-culture within English society. The cynicism explored by *Blackadder* is often there too in the poetry. It is clear in Wilfred Owen's 'Parable of the Old Man and the Young', and again it is couched in religious images. Using the story of Abraham and Isaac the poem ends:

Lo! an angel called him out of heaven,
Saying, lay not thy hand upon the lad,
Neither do anything to him. Behold,
A ram, caught in the thicket by its horns;
Offer the Ram of Pride instead of him.
But the old man would not so, but slew his son,
And half the seed of Europe, one by one.[19]

Here is a cynicism of a most sophisticated sort and it is clear that similar attitudes percolated throughout the military during the Great War. This was to leave its mark upon the churches, and not least the Church of England, whose establishment firmly linked it with those who were responsible both for the conflict itself and for the administration of the war. At the same time such cynicism would take its toll in the realm of belief. If the ordering of society and the purposefulness of history were now in question, then this automatically called into question other 'givens'. Who had so ordered society? If history was seemingly purposeless, then what did that say more broadly about the nature of human existence and some form of providence or teleology? This is explored with great sensitivity and perception by Alan Wilkinson in his study of *The Church of England and the First World War*.[20]

The questions of purpose and meaning are of particular significance, and were often made still more difficult for the Anglican chaplains. With their clear view of sacramental theology, and with a systematic ecclesiology, Roman Catholic chaplains were generally clear about their tasks. They were there to offer pastoral care which was focused in saying mass and in performing the sacrament of extreme unction, or the 'last rites' as it is popularly known. For Anglican clergy the position was less clear. They were dealing potentially with more people, but with vast numbers of nominal Anglicans. Furthermore, the focus upon the sacraments was by no means universally understood by the men, nor indeed always by the chaplains themselves. Without some sort of clear strategy, and a strong personality and sense of purpose, the Church of England clergy could easily be lost. Geoffrey Studdert-Kennedy, popularly known as 'Woodbine Willie', was the outstanding exception to this rule. Wilkinson writes:

> Studdert-Kennedy began the war with a simple, even blood-thirsty patriotism; but the experience of war at first hand forced him to discard, even to loathe, such views. At a popular, but deeply felt level (unlike academic theologians, he really was in touch with ordinary men), he explored most of the central themes for theology, ethics, and spirituality. Is God beyond or involved with the suffering world? . . . Does the cross make sense of suffering? How are we to understand the bible, the boundaries of the Church, sexual ethics, the eucharist, heaven and hell, the unseen and unrecognised Christ who is present in acts of human compassion as well as in the sufferings of the world?[21]

When Studdert-Kennedy prematurely died, between the wars, the streets of Worcester were lined with people to follow his funeral procession. By his outstanding and effective ministry he pointed up what was happening in the transformation effected by the Great War. It was his ability to minister unselfconsciously to men at all levels, his ability in his dialogue poetry to communicate directly and effectively that made him such a compelling figure. So he wrote:

> God, I hate this splendid vision – all its splendour is a lie,
> Splendid fools see splendid folly, splendid mirage born to die . . .
> . . . And I hate the God of Power on his hellish heavenly throne,
> Looking down on rape and murder, hearing little children moan
> . . .
> . . . God, the God I love and worship, reigns in sorrow on the
> Tree,

Broken, bleeding, but unconquered, very God of God to me.
All that showy pomp of splendour, all that sheen of angels' wings,
Was but borrowed from the baubles that surround our earthly
kings.[22]

Studdert-Kennedy had seen beyond the cynicism, but had seen
too the effects of the rasping, searing lens which was the Great
War and which would leave lasting changes upon English and
European culture. If the Church was to appeal to the hearts of
the people, then first of all it had to be perceptive of this vast
change in consciousness. People had now seen backstage, so to
speak: the old ordering of society was now contingent stage
scenery and little else. People needed a more subtle and credible
sense of purpose in human existence. Studdert-Kennedy proved
that the gospel still had a transforming power, but it required a
new sense of how the world is – 'Never such innocence before
or since . . . Never such innocence again.' In a nutshell, the Great
War marked the end of an existential innocence that could never
be recaptured. Studdert-Kennedy saw this and saw that by ignor-
ing it the Church would lose track of its own sense of purpose,
let alone the hearts of the English people.

*

The effects of the Great War upon the future stability of Europe
are well known. The exaggerated reparations expected of Germany
agreed at the Treaty of Versailles led to both bitterness and
instability within Germany. This, combined with the collapse of
the international monetary system in the late 1920s and early
1930s, provided the seedbed for revolution, nurtured and exploited
so effectively by Adolf Hitler and his confrères. Alongside this
destabilization there arose a real fear of the effects of another
European or world war. The 1914–18 conflict had devastated
a complete generation in France, England and Germany. Most
people had little appetite for further military adventurism.
Appeasement was in the air. Chamberlain and the valueless
Munich Agreement were not idiosyncratic within the inter-war
years, but largely representative of a prevailing mood. Furthermore,
it would be wrong to see this response as simply a matter of
pragmatism or cowardice. Principled attitudes and convictions

underpinned appeasement and the determination to avoid war. Nowhere was this clearer than from within the churches.

Dick (H. R. L.) Sheppard is an interesting case in point. Sheppard was to become one of the Anglican heroes of the inter-war years. His ministry at St Martin-in-the-Fields in London, and his exemplary contribution as one of the first 'radio parsons', assured him of certain fame, and not just within the churches. Sheppard had himself, for a very brief period, been a chaplain in the Great War and had effectively worn himself out in the process. Nevertheless, he did not lose his sense of vision. So, in lyrical tones, he set out his vision for St Martin-in-the-Fields when he went there. At his induction he reflected:

> I stood on the west steps and saw what this church would be to the life of the people. There passed me, into its warm inside, hundreds and hundreds of all sorts of people, going up to the temple of their Lord with all their difficulties, trials and sorrows. I saw it full of people, dropping in at all hours of the day and night ... And they said only one thing: 'This is our home. This is where we are going to learn the love of Jesus Christ.'[23]

As Alan Wilkinson points out in his book describing this period within the life of the churches, Sheppard had a remarkable capacity to identify with the weak and underprivileged, even though he himself came from an upper-middle-class background. Wilkinson writes:

> Sheppard's gospel was that God in Jesus had revealed himself as vulnerable love. Christianity was about Jesus. Like Raven, he believed that imitating Jesus was the essence of Christian discipleship, whereas non-pacifists explicitly or implicitly denied that we can resolve all questions by asking 'What would Jesus do?'[24]

It was effectively Sheppard who founded the Peace Pledge Union. In October 1934 a letter from him was published in the press, asking people to support the pledge: 'We renounce war, and never again, directly or indirectly, will we support or sanction another.' Out of this, in May 1936, issued the Peace Pledge Union supported by an impressive mixture of clergy, writers and other intellectuals including C. E. M. Joad, A. A. Milne, Charles Raven,

Donald Soper, George MacLeod, Vera Brittain, George Lansbury, Bertrand Russell and Siegfried Sassoon. The peak of its membership was in 1940, when it had some 136,000. The Union was just one of a number of initiatives, but it did exemplify the mood of the times and its rooting in a real moral commitment to peace and the avoidance of further conflict. This mood, however, was not to last. Indeed, although the Peace Pledge Union had a significant membership in 1940, the actual number of Christian pacifists at the time of the outbreak of war was fewer than 16,000 in total.

This is, of course, hardly surprising in the face of Hitler's tyranny and of the threat to Europe and democracy more widely. Even Chamberlain, who almost exemplified appeasement, was driven to declare war on Germany in September 1939. Ultimately, not only would Christians be caught up into the conflict, but there would be individual acts of both courage and extreme resistance. Dietrich Bonhoeffer's complicity in tyrannicide, through his part in the Stauffenberg plot to kill Hitler, is the most celebrated example. Hitler's war turned out to be a very different sort of war, not only on account of the new weaponry, but also because of the palpable moral evil against which the Allies were pitted. The poetry of the Second World War was of a very different register to that of the Great War. There were other reasons for this too. One was the terrible plight of the Jews. In prescient lines, W. H. Auden wrote his 'Refugee Blues' in March 1939:

> Say this city has ten million souls,
> Some are living in mansions, some are living in holes:
> Yet there's no place for us, my dear, yet there's no place for us...
>
> Saw a poodle in a jacket fastened with a pin.
> Saw a door opened and a cat let in:
> But they weren't German Jews, my dear, but they weren't German Jews...
>
> Stood on a great plain in the falling snow;
> Ten thousand soldiers marched to and fro:
> Looking for you and me, my dear, looking for you and me.[25]

Then too there was the irony that out of two decades of talk of appeasement and pacifism, of a time perhaps more determined to avoid war than ever before, still the nations of Europe, and latterly the world, found themselves engulfed in yet a greater conflict

still. Here is Sidney Keyes, who himself died in 1943 in the Desert
Campaign in North Africa. He calls his lines simply 'War Poet':

> I am the man who looked for peace and found
> My own eyes barbed.
> I am the man who grasped for words and found
> An arrow in my hand.
> I am the builder whose firm walls surround
> A slipping land.
> When I grow sick or mad
> Mock me not nor chain me:
> When I reach for the wind
> Cast me not down:
> Though my face is a burnt book
> And a wasted town.[26]

One of the single greatest ironies of Hitler's war was the
parallel level of social ferment throughout Europe, and notably
in England. The Great War had been styled as 'the war to end
all wars', but the majority emerged from it baffled, cynical or
disappointed about what it might have achieved for human
civilization. Herbert Read, a survivor of the earlier conflict, wrote
'To a Conscript of 1940'. It included this stanza:

> We think we gave in vain. The world was not renewed.
> There was hope in the homestead and anger in the streets
> But the old world was restored and we returned
> To the dreary field and workshop, and the immemorial feud
> Of rich and poor.[27]

As we have seen, at a deeper level the old world was not restored.
There was an irremediable loss of existential innocence. At the
political and social level, however, Read was right. The 1926
General Strike, the collapse of the dollar and the 'great depression' signalled further misery, and most notably for the poor.
England remained a stratified society despite the way in which
the Great War revealed the emptiness of the class system.
And so it was during the Second World War that the seeds of a
new order began to germinate and grow. William Beveridge
produced his report upon which the 'welfare state' would be
modelled. William Temple, successively Archbishop of York and
Canterbury, was a key collaborator. Temple, himself a classical
product of the upper-middle class and son of a former

Archbishop of Canterbury, now pressed for, and in some manner even began to exemplify, a commitment to a more egalitarian society.[28] Here was the Church identifying with the hearts of the English people and working for their social health as well as their metaphysical redemption. But was it too late?

In 1944 R. A. Butler unveiled his Education Bill, which presaged the broadening of secondary education to include all. It relied still on the dual system with the Church (and most notably the Church of England) as a key partner in the enterprise; regrettably, however, the Church of England never realized its potential in secondary education in the same way that it had committed and involved itself in 1902 and thereafter in elementary education, as it was then known. Two generations later, with the Dearing Report, it would seek to make up lost ground – but again, was it too late? This interrelating of Christianity and 'the social order' (to use William Temple's phrase) is the key issue in this period in terms of the Church's hold over the hearts of the English people. No longer could one assume that the social reformers of the Labour movement had their hearts truly fixed upon God. Perceptively, Clement Attlee noted of Lord Halifax, a well-known and most pious Anglican: 'Queer bird, Halifax. Very humorous, all hunting and Holy Communion.'[29] Later, talking to his biographer, Attlee was asked:

Harris: Would you say you were an agnostic?
Attlee: I don't know.
Harris: Is there an after-life, do you think?
Attlee: Possibly.[30]

The ground, then, had shifted. In the period from 1918 to 1945 (and in Britain, one would argue, from 1945 to 1951) a further innocence became eroded. Somehow this was the ending of a political and social innocence. In the 1930s, despite the terrifying and transforming lens of the Great War, politics remained unregenerate. The ferment between 1939 and 1948, both in war and in domestic politics, changed that irreversibly. The dénouement began to be played out most dramatically with the social revolution effected by the Labour government of 1945–51. Undoubtedly, Christian theology and moral principles were still there interwoven. R. H. Tawney was a key figure; Tom Driberg, Stafford Cripps and others were seminal influences too, as indeed was William Temple.[31] Now it was the turn of politicians – never such innocence again. Did the emergence of the welfare state characterize a further distancing of the hearts of the people from the gospel of Jesus Christ? Had the social impact of the Christian faith now been handed over to the state? This was part of the secularization thesis. The events of the past 25 years cast considerable doubt on such an analysis.

*

Having begun with theology in the crisis of modernism and then moved into broader movements of culture, the later twentieth century brings both these together in two rather different ways. So, for example, the cultural ferment of the 1960s had its impact upon theology. If one of the catch-phrases of the 1960s was 'doing one's own thing', then that was reflected in a broader individualism and subjectivism throughout society. It was the beginning of what is now often dubbed 'post-modern' culture. There is no doubting the outpouring of a creative impulse in this decade, but it is also interesting to see how swiftly that came to a close, and indeed how sharply it was criticized from a number of quarters in the years that followed. Certainly there was a frothiness about some of the creative outpourings, but there was also a real attempt in theology to understand what was then described as 'secularization'. Theological engagement was still possible within an optimistic climate, and it was this that gave birth in England to what became known as 'South Bank theology'. Within the Church of England, Mervyn Stockwood presided over the diocese of Southwark with great panache and charisma. Southwark pioneered the first ordination training course to happen outside the walls of a theological college. John Robinson brought together Tillich, Bonhoeffer and Bultmann in *Honest to God*;[32] the *Observer*, which was short of copy that week, included a headline implying that traditional images of God must go. This made the so-called radical bishop's book one of the bestsellers in theology of the twentieth century.

South Bank theology, however, extended more widely than this. Stockwood had the courage and imagination to appoint a series of able and interesting suffragan bishops. David Sheppard,

Test cricketer and director of east London's Mayflower Centre, pressed home the case for a 'bias to the poor', both in his time at Woolwich and later in Liverpool. Hugh Montefiore, fresh from Great St Mary's in Cambridge, also raised the intellectual temperature in a variety of controversial reflections. Hinting that Jesus could have been homosexual, he related the gospel to social issues. The optimism of the sixties, with the hope inspired by John F. Kennedy in the USA and in Harold Wilson's 'white heat of technology' in the UK, helped fuel a theological energy on both sides of the Atlantic. Some of this energy came from unexpected quarters. So, 'Death of God theology', with its roots in the New World, actually drew its nourishment from the Old World dogmatic writings of Karl Barth. Interestingly enough, some of the same issues which surrounded the crisis over the Catholic Modernists resurfaced. 'Transcendence' had been so emphasized by some Barthians that God became meaningless for people's lives, hence the writings of Thomas Altizer, Paul van Buren and even Harvey Cox.[33] 'Death of God theology' is now seen as a past and historical phenomenon to such a degree that it has become an entry in dictionaries of theology![34]

Despite the criticisms since poured out upon these various initiatives, there was a real attempt in each case to engage people with the Christian faith. Often these attempts would be directly through theological discussion. Many have since argued (in a way which parallels some of the earlier criticisms of Catholic Modernism) that these attempts were destined to fail since there was too eager an embracing of different forms of 'rationalism' leading down a path towards 'theological reductionism'. There is not sufficient space here to analyse each attempt at cultural accommodation, but certainly the 'Death of God enterprise' has itself now died. John Robinson's work aimed to popularize research that had been fairly regularly embraced by the theological community at the time. It is probably reasonable to argue that had some of the theological analysis been extended and deepened, the churches would have benefited in better understanding some of the difficulties which have since been encountered in living and proclaiming the gospel. Certainly it is true to say that the secularization thesis has been discredited in some of its key aspects by the persistence and growth of religious groups both within and beyond Christianity.[35]

Alongside pure theology, however, ran those attempts to engage again more effectively with social issues, but starting with the Christian gospel. David Sheppard and Hugh Montefiore have already been mentioned. They stood within a tradition which had a long and noble history on the other aside of the Atlantic, tracing its roots to Walter Rauschenbusch and the 'social gospel'. Later, Reinhold Niebuhr had generated his own distinctive 'Christian Realism' which influenced not only theologians and church leaders (including William Temple), but also politicians – from John F. Kennedy in the USA to R. A. Butler and Tony Benn in the UK. Alongside this should be mentioned the work of Ted Wickham, and the development of 'industrial mission'.[36] As the work of Wickham suggests, spiritual discipline and Christian spirituality would also be affected by these attempts to re-engage with the hearts of ordinary people. Douglas Rhymes took Harvey Cox's theme of secularization and applied it directly to prayer.[37] Sadly, there was a real sense of all these attempts being passé almost before the decade had ended.

If, then, in the second part of the twentieth century this engagement with secularization was one key strand, the other has been that which relates to globalization and an increasing multi-culturalism on both sides of the Atlantic. This had its first clear theological impact in Britain with the work of John Hick in the 1970s. Hick argued that just as in science there had been a Copernican Revolution, so a similar revolution has happened within religion. No longer was Christianity the sole religious tradition, even for Christian theologians. Instead of all the religions revolving around the planet Christianity, God now became the centre or the sun, with the great religions orbiting around his divine essence.[38] Since then (and notably with the rise of Islam) a whole new literature has developed.[39] This shift too has required Christian faith to review how it relates to contemporary society. One might argue that each of these two engagements has marked the end of any sense of religious innocence.

*

The twentieth century, we have argued, then, has been a period of receding innocence in one area after another of society, culture and intellectual discourse. The collapse of theological innocence with the Catholic Modernists, then the collapse of existential and later political innocence, finally gives way to a collapse in religious innocence. None of these has left the Christian Church untouched, yet each has also seen the churches in different ways trying to make contact with the hearts of those they fear they may have lost. Larkin wrote of the Great War:

> Never such innocence
> Never before or since . . .
> Never such innocence again.

It may be that it is in responding to the disappearances of each of these innocences that the Christian Church might begin to discover once again the way to people's hearts. Why are things so different on the western side of the Atlantic – is it that some of these innocences have positively survived, or is it that in that New World they were never created or received?

6

And into a brave new world?

The cuttings were mainly about *Humanae Vitae* and its
repercussions . . . The books in the rucksack were paperbacks on sociology, psychology, philosophy, sexuality, com-
parative religion. Austin felt that he had a lot of reading
to catch up on – too much. His head was a buzzing hive
of awakened but directionless ideas. There was Freud who
said that we must acknowledge our own repressed desires,
and Jung who said that we must recognise our archetypal
patterning, and Marx who said we must join the class struggle and Marshall McLuhan who said we must watch more
television. There was Sartre who said that man was absurd
though free and Skinner who said he was a bundle of con-
ditioned reflexes and Chomsky who said he was a sentence-
generating organism and Wilhelm Reich who said he was
an orgasm-having organism. Each book that Austin read
seemed to him totally persuasive at the time, but they
couldn't all be right. And which were most easily reconcil-
able with faith in God? For that matter, what was God? Kant
said that he was the essential presupposition of moral
action, Bishop Robinson said he was the ground of our
being, and Teilhard de Chardin said he was the Omega
Point. Wittgenstein said, whereof we cannot speak, thereof
we must remain silent – an aphorism in which Austin
Brierley found great comfort.[1]

Austin Brierley is David Lodge's liberated Roman Catholic priest,
a chaplain at the University of London in the 1960s where 'doing
your own thing' was a watchword, and where there seemed to
be a seemingly unhaltable drift towards relativism. One could
argue that the more recent coinage 'post-modernism' is but a
development of that same tendency. As the twentieth century

heralded an existential loss of innocence, so was that lost innocence swiftly becoming some form of Huxley's 'Brave New World'? Lodge's literary excursion into the enthusiasms of the sixties is not merely whimsical, for it identifies at the very least confusion, and at the worst a sense of religious meaninglessness. The feeling is one of a society or culture that has somehow pulled free from its moorings. Does any objectivity survive? If so does it have anything to do with a European civilization founded upon the Christian faith? Has God become marginal to people's lives? And, as Austin Brierley asks: 'For that matter, what was God?'

Into this bubbling cauldron was tipped the theory of secularization. On one level it was not a theory at all. It was simply an acknowledgement of changes in society, which could trace their roots at least into the last quarter of the nineteenth century. Until that time much of the social structure of society had been provided by the Church. Hospitals remain conspicuous in being dedicated to saints. Education, patchy as it was, owed much to initiatives from both the established Church and Dissent. With the move towards the cities and the exponential growth in population, however, the churches could no longer sustain the sort of growth necessary if adequate education and health care were to be provided. So the 1870 Forster Education Act, and then the 1902 Act, expanded provision by opting for the 'dual system'.[2] Although this spoke of a Church–State partnership, it also marked the beginning of the state taking responsibility for infrastructures in a number of walks and departments of daily life. Lloyd George's first administration added to this with the very beginnings of welfare provision. In other areas, health for example, state intervention came much later. It was the 1945–51 Labour government which moved things on very significantly by setting up a 'welfare state' largely on the lines set out in the Beveridge Report. Aneurin Bevan, the chief political architect of the National Health Service, effectively 'nationalized' the hospitals and persuaded the British Medical Association and the other key medical societies to co-operate with the state in setting up a comprehensive and 'free on entry' health care service for the whole of the nation.[3] This shift towards state intervention, where the churches became more peripheral within the overall provisions than they had been in the past, was one understanding of the term 'secularization'.

Interestingly enough, even within this understanding of secularization, there has been something of a reversal. The allegedly non-interventionist approach to government, pioneered by Margaret Thatcher in the United Kingdom and Ronald Reagan in the United States of America, has effected significant changes throughout the world.[4] State intervention has retreated in a number of the developed nations, and often this has been accompanied by a deliberate encouragement to the voluntary sector to shoulder responsibilities for different 'social programmes'. In Britain there has also been encouragement from the government to the churches to play a still fuller part in the state educational provision, and notably in the secondary sector; the Church of England has responded to this with some vigour.[5] Indeed, the intention is to double the number of secondary schools as a result of this initiative. All this indicates significant retreat from this element of secularization in the last quarter of the twentieth century.

The second and broader understanding of secularization is effectively more sociological in character. Put most sharply by one of the classical commentators: 'Secularisation is the process of social change in which religion loses its social significance.'[6]

Analysis of this process has taken a variety of forms. Effectively the process of secularization is seen as a product of the Enlightenment. The Enlightenment itself caused people to differentiate between sacred and secular; reason became separated from faith. This is not the place to engage in a detailed analysis of the Enlightenment and its interpreters. Instead, realistically, one can describe a tendency to separate out the rules of truth, science and human behaviour from earlier assumed 'theological roots'. To some degree the churches and a developing world of professional theologians implicitly accepted this analysis, and most notably in biblical studies. It was not simply that the Bible could be studied using the new tools made available through Enlightenment thought. Instead, it was that the implications of such study were seen by certain scholars as driving an ever-widening wedge between sacred and secular views of the world. David Friedrich Strauss' classical analysis *The Life of Jesus* is one example.

With regard to society, it was argued, increasing numbers of people had lost their sense of piety and religion, and so their understanding of the world was correspondingly divorced from God and providence. It is, of course, undeniably the case that the processes of industrialization and urbanization have distanced the majority of the population from the effects of times and seasons upon the growth of crops, and thus upon the immediate production of food. Food now is mediated to us by a complex processing and retailing chain. In a rural society the sense of God having a direct impact upon the flourishing of the community was always there. Now providence impinges less obviously. Nevertheless, this is a shift that stretches back well into the nineteenth century and was unlikely to have taken until the 1960s to show its full impact. So, Owen Chadwick writes:

> Something happened to religious people which affected their attitude to the world; I do not say for better or worse, for gain or for loss; a change in attitude remotely comparable to the change when Greek philosophy became available to the schoolmen, or the change when the Renaissance altered men's attitudes to humanity. We may have less sense of providence in our lives.[7]

Even Chadwick here begs the question of what we might mean by 'religious people'. The reference to people 'being religious' rather than 'not being religious' is very much a modern coinage. When people came to pray after the death of Princess Diana or the horrors of the destruction of New York's twin towers, they were often heard saying, to either a priest or a journalist: 'I'm not a religious person, but I just had to come into the cathedral and pray.' Does 'religious' here simply mean 'churchgoing'? If so, then, the fall off in churchgoing is hardly a new phenomenon, even if it was accentuated in the later twentieth century. For it is also true that the assumed falling away from piety of parents and grandparents has a much longer history than is often assumed. Many families can trace back to their grandparents (born in the 1880s) only the very loosest 'folk-religion'.

One of the most acute commentators on the process is, as we saw earlier, Grace Davie. In reflecting upon a number of recent sociological studies, and the trend issuing from them, she writes:

> this series of publications forms part of a continuing reappraisal of the place of religion in the modern world ... More specifically it calls into question at least some aspects of the process known as secularization, notably the assumption

that secularization is a necessary part of modernization and that as the world modernized it would – all other things being equal – be likely to secularize.[8]

Elsewhere she demonstrates that some writers still believe the secularization thesis to hold true. She quotes Steve Bruce: 'Individualism threatened the communal basis of religious belief and behaviour, while rationality removed many of the purposes of religion and rendered many of its beliefs implausible.'[9]

In Davie's words, the sacred canopy, according to Bruce, had begun to unravel, and that process has continued further as the years have passed. One of the other key critics arguing still for the secularization thesis is Callum Brown. He writes: 'It took several centuries . . . to convert Britain to Christianity, but it has taken less than forty years for the country to forsake it.'[10]

Since 1963, he notes:

a formerly religious people have entirely forsaken organised Christianity in a sudden plunge into a truly secular con- dition . . . What emerges is a story not merely of Church decline, but of the end of Christianity as a means by which men and women, as individuals, construct their identities and their sense of 'self'.[11]

This Brown attributes largely to the falling away of women in Britain in the realm of religious observance. Grace Davie dis- putes this, arguing that other social organizations have collapsed even more spectacularly when they depended upon male domin- ance; she cites particularly trade unions and political parties.[12] Davie's instinct, however, is that secularization theory is running out of steam, both through its own internal inconsistencies and also in the face of religion's persistence – and even growth – in many parts of the world. Drawing on her own research, and that of David Martin[13] and Peter Berger, she effectively argues that the secularization thesis is effectively reversed. In the USA, religion remains vibrant. Grace Davie writes:

So what happens to the argument about relativism breed- ing secularity? In the US it simply hasn't happened. What has emerged in its place has been a healthy and competi- tive market of religious institutions, some of which appear to be thriving more vigorously than others.[14]

All this recent research, and indeed the empirical shifts in the way in which religions (and not just Christianity) have continued to thrive, requires us to review the analyses of the 1960s, and reactions to them. David Martin notes, for example: 'Crucially I argue that instead of regarding secularization as a once-for-all unilateral process, one might rather think in terms of successive Christianizations followed or accompanied by recoils.'[15]

If these theses are now less convincing, in the light of contemporary sociological evidence, then how should we view the reactions of churches and theologians to the then perceived process of secularization? For the theory of secularization, expounded in the 1960s, provoked immediate reaction in the world of theology and the churches. Some reactions were defensive, but others embraced this secularizing analysis with enthusiasm, seeing it as a welcome means of liberating the Christian world from an oppressive and, at times, unimaginative past. One of the high priests of secularization in the 1960s, if that term is not too soaked in irony, was Harvey Cox. Summarizing the spirit of the age, Cox wrote: 'Secularisation is the name for an ideology, a new closed world-view which functions very much like a new religion.'[16]

Instead of offering a critique of secularism in the light of secularization, however, Cox, along with many others, embraced the sociological analysis and attempted to offer a response and an accommodation from the point of view of Christian theology. So he argued:

> The fact that urban–secular man is incurably and irreversibly pragmatic, that he is less and less concerned with religious questions, is in no sense a disaster. It means that he is shedding the lifeless cuticles of the mythological and ontological periods, and stepping into the functional age. He is leaving behind the styles of the tribe and the town, and becoming a technopolitan man.[17]

This leads Cox to title his final chapter 'To speak in a secular fashion of God'. This chapter is a fascinating mélange of unashamed secularized Christianity and also a critique of some whom he believes have embraced the secular in inappropriate ways. So of Paul van Buren, he writes:

He [van Buren] then goes on to a discussion of the logical structure of the language of faith, in the course of which he says that modern man has difficulties with any word which refers to what he calls the 'transcendent'. I think at this point van Buren is wrong. The problem is not bad language.[18]

Further on, however, using language that was picked up by others in still more radical ways, Cox argues:

But how do we name the God who is not interested in our fasting and cultic adoration but asks for acts of mercy? It is too early to say for sure, but it may well be that our English word *God* will have to die, corroborating in some measure Nietzsche's apocalyptic judgement that 'God is dead'.[19]

Cox continues, then, to protest about outdated tribal and cultic views of God. He is keen to engage with a political agenda and to move to a form of Christian theology and life which embraces the world and an agenda which the world presents. He does so in a manner which all too easily fails to challenge some of the most elementary perceptions of the world. Although he is unhappy with van Buren's apparent wholesale rejection of the transcendent, nevertheless it is a celebration of immanence that Cox is keen to sponsor. Here we see surfacing just the sorts of problems warned of in the modernist crisis. Daly makes clear in his analysis of that crisis that most of the writers dubbed with the 'modernist' label were keen to preserve an appropriate balance, or even tension, in relation to God's presence as it can be encountered in our experience and that element of the divine which ever calls us on. As we have seen, Tyrrell was very keen indeed to claim transcendence for Jesus Christ, and attacked the Liberal Protestants for failing to do this. It is not entirely unfair to see some of the secularizing theologians of the 1960s as the true inheritors of the more extreme immanentist elements within nineteenth-century Liberal Protestantism.

In his later writings Cox recanted, to some degree, his argument in *The Secular City*. Nevertheless, his perception of the forces of secularization in that book and his prescribed responses to those forces characterize the reactions of theologians in that period fairly accurately. So, the argument went: if the hearts of the people were not further to be lost, then we must seek out those hearts in the brave new world of a secularized order. In the United Kingdom, Douglas Rhymes responded to Cox's analysis by offering a new spirituality which attempted to enfold the secular.[20] Prayer was not restricted to formal times and within church buildings; in a secular world it must happen whenever and wherever one found oneself. Prayer should also relate to political and social realities and thus took on the immanentist flavour of Cox's theological analysis.

With its emphasis upon an urbanized world, the theory of secularization had its influence on both sides of the Atlantic. In Britain the so-called 'South Bank theology', of which Douglas Rhymes was one exponent, was the most obvious excrescence of secularized theology. The most remarkable example of this was the reaction to Bishop John Robinson's paperback *Honest to God*.[21] John Robinson's book was part of a series of paperbacks, and so might have expected to sell modestly in 'theologically educated' circles. As we noted earlier, on the Sunday before its publication the sub-editors of the *Observer* Sunday newspaper chose the headline 'Our Image of God Must Go'. Adding this headline to the fact that the book had been written by a bishop made it theological dynamite. Within the first few months it sold nearly 400,000 copies, and ultimately it has sold more than one million. Even at the time of writing, news has just filtered through to say that the rights for publication of the book have recently been sold to a Czech publisher for the book to be published for the first time in that language, in addition to the many other foreign-language editions already published. All this, and it is now some 43 years on.

Is it fair to see South Bank theology and *Honest to God* as part of the secularization debate? What, indeed, was *Honest to God* about? Effectively, the book was a concise analysis and bringing together of some of the key themes of the writings of three notable theologians – Rudolf Bultmann, Dietrich Bonhoeffer and Paul Tillich. 'The ground of our being' was a phrase taken from Tillich, but traceable ultimately to St Augustine of Hippo. Although its original provenance was Patristic, nevertheless it characterized much of the existentialist thinking of Paul Tillich's theology. It replaced, in John Robinson's view, some of the crude anthropomorphic pictures currently held of God. 'The man for others' was a phrase plucked from the writings of Bonhoeffer.

Again, it focused on Bonhoeffer's own particular approach, reaching out beyond formulaic and stereotypical views of religion. In this context it also resonated with those who were arguing for a more immanently based Christian gospel. It spoke to the secularizers; it spoke to the secular city. Jesus is seen as reaching out to everyone in their own existential situation. Other chapters, too, breathed a freshness through their titles alone. 'A new morality' hinted at situation ethics. 'The end of theism' brought with it a deliberately polemical feel. Robinson's discussion of Rudolf Bultmann – a New Testament theologian commenting on another New Testament theologian – referred to Bultmann's programme of 'demythologization'. The myths of the biblical writers now needed to be clothed with the myths of our own time, be they Freudian, Jungian or Marxian myths, set in the context of a Christian critique.

Robinson's book, then, was hardly popular theology in any journalistic sense. It did, however, seek to generate a real debate about how contemporary Christians and theologians could now talk about God, and how they could articulate a vision of God's presence in the world. It did so using the language available at the time and speaking from the context of the inner city, from whence so much talk of secularization had sprung. In an essay following up the debate on the book, Robinson wrote specifically about secularization and the mythological, the metaphysical, the supernatural and then the religious. He prefaces this with a brief discussion about the meaning of secularization. He reflects:

> I believe that the process of secularisation represents the same kind of shift in man's whole way of looking at the world as that which marked the transition from the Middle Ages to the Renaissance. That is to say, it is of its nature something towards which the Christian faith as such is neutral. Or, rather, the Christian must welcome and respond to it as a God-given fact, as the world-view within which Christ has to be made flesh for modern man.
>
> This will not be easy for the Church, because secularisation stands amongst other things for a revolt against three ways of viewing the world, and probably four, which have been intimately bound up in the past with the presentation of the Christian gospel.[22]

Thereafter follows his analysis of the four words noted above. Here, then, Robinson does tackle the issue of secularization head on. Indeed, he ends this essay by noting:

> secular man is just as much inside the Church as out of it, and just as much inside myself. Indeed my book was born out of the fact that I knew myself to be a man committed, without possibility of return, to modern twentieth century secular society. It was written out of the belief that both these convictions must be taken with equal seriousness and that they cannot be incompatible.[23]

The issue which is paramount here is: did the Church and theologians, in their response to the secularization debate in the 1960s, so react as to divert the theological response too immediately? If the process of the divorcing of much of society from traditional understandings of providence had been continuing for more than a century, then that process would have had an impact over a number of decades. Secularization, as described in the 1960s debate, would not have been a sudden phenomenon. It was instead one way of describing a shift whose roots go back a long way, not only into Enlightenment thought but also into demographic changes wrought by industrialization and urbanization. So, put rather crudely, did theologians and the Church over-react to the secularization debate and at certain points, unnecessarily and unhelpfully, de-sacralize the gospel?

*

John Robinson's infamous book (as it became seen), and reactions to it, is as good a place to start as any in attempting to respond to these questions. First, a little more on the book itself. How has the theology which it attempted to popularize fared within the intellectual market place in the decades which have followed? Theology and theologians, rather like artists, musical composers, authors and poets, are a prey to fashion and changes in fashion. In addition to this they often suffer immediately after their deaths, and enter, so to speak, a critical eclipse. In twentieth-century music, then, the Impressionists, Vaughan Williams and even Benjamin Britten suffered this sort of eclipse perhaps a decade or two after their deaths. It was only later that their true critical greatness has come to be appreciated.

This has certainly been the case with theologians, and, among those popularized by Robinson, most notably with both Rudolf Bultmann and Paul Tillich. Bultmann remains one of the giants of twentieth-century biblical theology. He was one of the creative synthesizers of critical study of the New Testament, following the pioneering work done in Germany in the nineteenth century. Most significant was his establishment of 'form criticism' as one of the key building blocks in understanding the origins of the first three (synoptic) Gospels.[24] By analysing the different 'forms' or genres within the Gospels, Bultmann was able to suggest a possible *Sitz im Leben* (situation in life) for the tiny sections or vignettes which make up the first three Gospels. The parable, miracle and dispute 'forms', he argued, originated as sermon-style material from within the early Church. Similarly, his remarkable commentary on the fourth Gospel was pioneering, and it remains a key resource for Johannine scholars still.[25] Neither of these analyses has passed without criticism, but his foundation work would remain seminal.

It is in his programme for 'demythologization' that his reputation has fared less well.[26] His argument that there are controlling myths which underpin a culture or society's self-understanding would now be widely accepted. Classical studies have revealed how ancient Greek civilization understood itself in the context of the gods of the Homeric epics of the *Odyssey* and the *Iliad*. Although that literature remains an essential and nourishing part of our culture, understood in its broad sense, the providence implied by the working of these gods is now seen as a myth specific to antiquity. Similarly, the linking of Christianity with the cult of the saints and of relics, and the interlocking of this with some traditions of magic, is no longer seen as an integral part of Christian belief.[27] That part of Bultmann's thesis, then, would be generally accepted. Bultmann was extremely sceptical about the amount of reliable historical material encountered in the Gospel narrative. He moves on to suggest that the mythical elements within the New Testament are best discarded in favour of an existential understanding. Christian myth must also be discarded in favour of an existential understanding. This understanding is dependent upon the writings of Martin

Heidegger. In the early to mid twentieth century, existentialism enjoyed a very considerable vogue. Often tracing its antecedents back to the Danish Christian philosopher Søren Kierkegaard, existentialism covered a wide spectrum. That spectrum ranged from avowedly atheistic approaches, including the writings of Jean-Paul Sartre and Albert Camus, through an uncommitted and agnostic group of philosophers (Heidegger would reside here), all the way across to Christian existentialists which included Bultmann, John Macquarrie and Paul Tillich. Bultmann's historical scepticism and his enthusiasm for an existentialist clothing of Christian theology have made him less fashionable two generations further on. His programme, which also sidelines much of the historical material, is seen as reductionist.

This brief analysis brings us to another of John Robinson's key writers, Paul Tillich. Tillich again had a panoramic approach to Christian theology. His sermons, rooted in his existentialism, were challenging.[28] They issued not only from his rich intellectual background, but had also been provoked by his need to leave Nazi Germany in the early 1930s. This personal experience lent an immediacy to his writings, caught up not only in his sermons but also in his shorter theological monographs.[29] These writings, alongside his systematic theological work[30] were coloured by a unique theological psychology. So the provocation to engage with religious belief was induced by what Tillich described as 'ontological shock'. Then one of his descriptions of God was ultimate concern. Even his use of the Augustinian phrase 'ground of our being' carried with it a twentieth-century theological overtone. This psychological overlay, combined with the existential matrix within which all was set, has led many critics to argue that Tillich's theological language is so elusive as to be suspect, or even meaningless. Nonetheless, Tillich's analysis of the human condition remains challenging. Whether his integrated constructive theological framework will be rehabilitated remains more uncertain.

All this suggests, then, that Robinson's eclectic theological response to the secularization debate is, so far, less convincing 40 years on and notably following the widespread critique of the secularization thesis itself. One further contributor, however, remains there for us to examine. Dietrich Bonhoeffer is arguably the best-known Christian martyr of the twentieth century. Hanged following his implication in the Stauffenberg plot to kill Adolf Hitler, Bonhoeffer has been one of the most influential, yet enigmatic, theologians of the last century. He was one of a group of German Christians who focused resistance to the Nazi regime before and during the Second World War. His work with George Bell, Bishop of Chichester, in trying to marshal the forces of resistance in Germany, and also to work for a negotiated peace, remains one of the seminal pieces of Christian witness within modern history.

None of this, however, was a purely pragmatic response. It was rooted in a profound, and on occasions, opaque theology; Bonhoeffer has been called as a witness by people from a great variety of theological and moral traditions in support of their cause.[31] A Lutheran pastor, Bonhoeffer had become an admirer of Karl Barth's 'neo-Orthodox' theology which was rooted firmly in *revelation*; Barth was opposed to 'natural theology', which assumed that humanity could deduce both the existence and the trajectory of God's providence through reason and, thus, through reflection upon the natural order. The tragedy of the Great War had convinced Barth that human fallenness had wiped out any ability to reason effectively and thus move towards Christian faith. Instead, Christ confronts us with God's challenge to the new life. Bonhoeffer moved on in his theological investigations, however, and began to engage with Bultmann's critique of earlier understandings of the Christian 'myth'. Ultimately, however, Bonhoeffer was his own man, and embraced neither of these two theologians, but instead came through an almost Hegelian dialectic to his own analysis of the human condition. From his prison cell he wrote of the emergence of a 'religionless Christianity'.[32] This did not mean, as many of the Christian responses in the 1960s to secularization implied, a wholesale rejection of the tradition or an overturning of worship, prayer and contemplation. Indeed, it was Bonhoeffer's adherence to that integrity of faith which secures him a place as a theologian of outstanding significance. He brought together theology, worship and Christian witness in a unique manner. The doctor at Flossenburg prison camp wrote this of Bonhoeffer's death:

On the morning of that day between five and six o'clock the prisoners, among them Admiral Canaris, General Osler

... and *Reichsgerichtsartzt* Sack were taken from their cells, and the verdicts of the court martial read out to them. Through the half open door in one of the huts I saw Pastor Bonhoeffer, before taking off his prison garb, kneeling on the floor praying fervently to his God. I was most deeply moved by the way this lovable man prayed, so devout, and so certain that God heard his prayer. At the place of execution, he again said a short prayer and then climbed the step to the gallows, brave and composed. His death ensued after a few seconds. In the almost fifty years that I worked as a doctor, I have hardly ever seen a man die so entirely submissive to the will of God.[33]

It was of such Christian witness, effectively, that Bonhoeffer wrote in his great book *Ethics*.[34] It is also this combination of witness, theological reflection and analysis of the human condition in the twentieth century that assures him of a lasting place in the Christian pantheon. Furthermore, Bonhoeffer's authenticity and integrity are two ingredients that are always essential if Christianity is to touch the hearts of the people. Of all the material in Robinson's book, and in his response to secularization theory, it is his adoption of Bonhoeffer which endures. Even here, however, we must be wary of the rather caricatured description of Bonhoeffer's analysis and theological position which emerged from the engagement of many theologians with secularization in the 1960s.

Robinson's book, therefore, now feels to be something of a period piece. Indeed, it is interesting that in a monograph reviewing *Honest to God*, 40 years later, there is no analysis whatsoever either of secularization or of Robinson's own attempt to engage with secularization as it was understood at the time. There are interesting essays on the language of theism and on Christology, but much of the rest either looks back to the events of the book's publication or considers whether there is an enduring message from the book. As Colin Buchanan rightly argues, the book made so much more of a splash because of the paucity of other news at that particular moment, and because of the chosen headline in the *Observer*.[35] However, in neither Buchanan's essay nor the essay looking at the book's legacy is there an analysis of the secularization crisis – as it might have been termed – nor indeed of Robinson's response to it. Robinson's response was, of course, that secularization was a revolt against certain ways of seeing the world. We have now seen how views of secularization have changed.

What precisely had Bonhoeffer seen secularization to be? Was there not something deeper still relating to issues of providence? Following the Enlightenment, sacred and secular had been separated as they never had been before. One of the most terrifying examples of this was in the French Revolution. In that case, morality had been wrenched from any links with an objective anchorage; a form of positivism took over. God was removed from the equation. The results of this were seen in both the bloodiness of the revolution itself and in the instability, disloyalty and anarchy that followed; the terrors of the Vendée were the direct sequel to the revolution. Indeed, in his analysis of secularization in the nineteenth century, Owen Chadwick notes:

> The word *secularisation* began as an emotive word, not far in its origins from the word *anticlericalism*. Sometimes it meant a freeing of the sciences, of learning, of the arts, from their theological origins or theological bias. Sometimes it meant the declining influence of the churches, or of religion, in modern society ... Modern sociologists (and others) have not always kept the word to this unemotional plane. Sometimes they have used it as a word of propaganda.[36]

It was, indeed, this very separation of religion and the secular that made it almost impossible for the churches in Germany to oppose Hitler. Bonhoeffer's point in pursuing what he called 'religionless Christianity' was precisely to address this: that is, to make certain that the gospel engaged with every aspect of living, and not with some supposedly *religious* part of it. Such an approach engages directly too with talk of people being 'religious' or not. It addresses the woman who prayed in church after the death of Princess Diana, but who declared herself not to be 'religious'. It may be that Bonhoeffer did have some vision of a religionless world. Certainly, that has not materialized in any literal sense. But Bonhoeffer's real message is that Jesus, in being 'the man for others', lived out true godliness within the same world which we inhabit. Bonhoeffer argued that:

God shouldn't be smuggled into some lost secret place, but that we should frankly recognise that the world, and people, have come of age, that we shouldn't run down man in his worldliness, but confront him with God at his strongest point.[37]

This seems to be an essential insight as we seek to touch the hearts of all with the Christian gospel. It is an insight also which needs to penetrate any theology of providence in the light of theories of secularization. Interestingly enough, Christianity has all too often sought to restrict God's presence to the extra-ordinary and to 'interventionist' events. This is a restrictive and exclusive picture of providence which coincides with a world which separates out phenomena (alongside all human experi-ence) into the *religious* and the *secular*. Avoiding such a crude distinction allows God's presence to be far more ubiquitous. Owen Chadwick writes:

> The question, whether the exceptional quality ascribed to events or things in the dawn of humanity was the only way to perception of the sacred? Was this movement from unusual to usual a deprivation, so that if all the world is supernatural nothing is supernatural and everything is dis-enchanted? Or was it an insight, like seeing that because Sunday is a holy day all days are holy days, or that because an altar is a holy table for a holy meal, all tables and all meals are holy?[38]

This, of course, reaches to the heart of a sacramental view of life, where God's presence is ubiquitous, but where the focuses of that presence are an essential element within religious experience, worship and practice. All this suggests that understanding secu-larization as the separation of the religious and secular (a differ-ent understanding from those set out earlier in this chapter) is a challenge to us. It is a challenge to live fully in the world, but to allow the Christian faith to remain sacramentally present through people's lives as well as through worship and prayer.[39]

Writing in the late 1950s or early 1960s, just as the secular-ization debate was beginning, W. H. Auden, who had himself now returned to an active Christian faith, meditates upon the death of Bonhoeffer, whose name had been so caught up in the

debate. In a most powerful poem focused on the cross and resurrection, Auden writes:

> Now, did He really break the seal
> And rise again? We dare not say;
> But conscious unbelievers feel
>   Quite sure of Judgment Day.
>
> Meanwhile a silence on the cross,
> As dead as we shall ever be,
> Speaks of some total gain or loss,
>   And you and I are free
>
> To guess from the insulted face
> Just what Appearances He saves
> By suffering in a public place
>   A death reserved for slaves.[40]

Too much commentary on Auden's poetry will only obscure
rather than clarify. The ambiguities stare us in the eye, and there
is not one iota of separation – secularization disappears like melt-
ing snow.

7

Circling them in or out?

———•◆•———

Many of our reflections so far have been historical and to some degree sociological. We have also tracked changes in the way in which the Church and wider society have related to each other through theological shifts within the Church or sometimes demographic changes within the English landscape. These shifts and changes, however, sometimes reveal particular approaches and attitudes which the Church and theologians have adopted as they have sought to relate the Christian gospel to the world in which they have found themselves. Sometimes these approaches have embraced wider society, and sometimes they have seen the Church operating in a more exclusive mode. So, should the Church opt for inclusivity or exclusivity? Much earlier on we reflected on the exclusion of Roman Catholic and Dissenters in the late sixteenth and seventeenth centuries:

> They drew a circle that shut me out –
> Heretic, rebel, a thing to flout.
> But love and I had the wit to win –
> We drew a circle that took them in.[1]

Edwin Markham's well-known epigram, which we encountered earlier, also focuses a debate which has never been far from the surface in the history of the Christian Church. Is the Church ineluctably counter-cultural or is it unavoidably shaped by the ambient culture? Is the Church ineluctably inclusive, an ever-enfolding community of redeemed sinners? Or is it the ark of the saved, a well-defended association of the saints? Contemporary debates about Christianity and sexuality, for example, sometimes claim that theology has eschewed any accommodation with culture. If the Church is to survive and proclaim the gospel, it must guard the deposit of faith infallibly preserved in Scripture and Tradition. Ralph Inge, sometime Dean of St Paul's, famously quipped: 'The Church which is married to the Spirit of the Age will be a widow in the next.' Inge was himself a 'modernist' in terms of theology but was nevertheless still keen to warn the Church of the dangers of an unconscious and uncritical alignment with the culture of the time. The sum of such arguments is to produce a *counter-cultural description* of the Church and of the Christian faith.

Our last chapter engaged with the debate about secularization and notably with that debate as it emerged in the 1960s, and then also with all the ensuing arguments throughout the last quarter of the twentieth century. But Austin Brierley in David Lodge's novel, whom we quoted earlier, and John Robinson in *Honest to God* were not merely facing issues of secularization. They were facing these issues in the context of the continuing debate about the Christian gospel and its relationship with the surrounding culture. In a later set of essays John Robinson effectively faces exactly this problem. Indeed, he is concerned precisely with this issue of the Church engaging with the wider world, with contemporary culture. So he writes: 'The conception of "being the Church", as opposed simply to "going to Church" is one that has brought new vision and vitality to many a congregation in recent years.'[2]

Robinson moves on to describe the dangers of isolating man-talk (using the exclusive language of the time) from God-talk, the Church from the world. He notes:

> The gospel *does* give men [sic] meaning and fulfilment in society, and, unless it is preached in terms of the particular content of this social salvation, it becomes irrelevant; but it tells them that this is to be had, not by seeking it, but by losing it, not by striving and works, but by faith and grace. 'Seek ye first the Kingdom of God and his righteousness and all these things shall be added unto you.'[3]

The danger of the Church becoming introverted or isolated from the ambient culture will never disappear; there will always remain an unavoidable tension. Arguments that the Church should be predominantly or even totally counter-cultural have reared their heads again and again. They remain with us today.

Indeed, it was not obvious, even in New Testament times, that the Church is a naturally and endemically counter-cultural organization, and that alone. A brief analysis of just one of these semi-proverbial phrases which appears in different forms throughout the synoptic (first three) Gospels shows how elusive is any final and conclusive doctrine relating the gospel to culture. Take, for example, the saying of Jesus which appears in Matthew (12.30). Here James is quoted as saying: 'He who is not with me is against me, and he who does not gather with me scatters.' The feel of this sentence is combative and it marks off the teaching of Jesus as distinctive and challenging. It occurs within a passage about the exorcism of demons in the name of Beelzebub, the prince of demons. The saying may originally have been independent from this passage[4] but it is clearly marking out the boundaries of the influences of evil and of Satan. The message is that one cannot be neutral in this particular battle.[5] This suggests that in Matthew's Gospel the Church already exists in an embryonic form and that it is important for people to know where the Church's boundaries lie. Luke 11.23 takes over the Matthean context in the dispute over exorcism and the note of exclusion remains.

The earliest form of this saying in the New Testament, however – that is, in Mark's Gospel – affirms almost precisely the opposite to what James is saying in the dispute over exorcism and Beelzebub in Matthew and Luke. In Mark 9.40 Jesus is reported as saying: 'For he who is not against us is for us' (or in some translations: 'For he who is not against us is on our side'). Here the saying comes also in quite a different context. It is separated from the Beelzebub dispute, which appears earlier in the Gospel (3.20–27); here there is no reference to this saying. Instead, in chapter 9, this different form of what otherwise sounds like a very similarly structured aphorism comes after an incident where there has been exorcising of demons in the name of Jesus. Surely this must be stopped? Jesus' response is to be permissive, even encouraging: 'Do not forbid him; for no one who does a mighty work in my name will be able soon after to speak evil of me' (Mark 9.39). So, to put it succinctly, he who is not against us is on our side. There is an inclusivity about Jesus' 'teaching' here in Mark. He draws a circle to take others in. Here is an example of the evangelist deliberately reporting Jesus working *with* at least one element within the surrounding culture. This saying in its various forms, then, was probably well known in the ancient world. Commentators remark upon the tolerance or inclusiveness of both the saying and the incident within which it occurs.[6]

What can be said, however, more generally about the New Testament and its relationship to its ambient culture? This in itself is an immensely complex question. It would be both perverse and naïve to imply that Jesus, in his mission, life and death, was never counter-cultural. It would be equally obtuse to argue this about the New Testament witness as a whole. The parting of the ways between Judaism and what eventually became Christianity, and then later the establishment of the Church, all bear witness to the prophetic and counter-cultural elements within Jesus' ministry and within the life of the embryonic post-apostolic Church. Nevertheless, even our brief worked example from the synoptic Gospels has indicated that there were clearly continuities too. Mark portrays Jesus offering an inclusive message at that point. This point has been made sharply by some New Testament critics in recent years in relation to the naïve contrasts that have often been made between Christianity and first-century Rabbinic Judaism.[7] Similar points might be made about Christianity and the background of Hellenistic thought.[8]

Even a fairly cursory analysis of the background to the New Testament and the sub-apostolic period raises this issue fairly sharply. Take, for example, the persistence of Gnosticism, both within and outside the embryonic Christian community. Gnosticism describes various systems of belief which claimed to impart a unique knowledge of God and of God's relation to the world and to humanity. It often also included a special knowledge of redemption which would be the possession only of those who had been initiated. They would form an intellectually and spiritually enlightened community, and through linking into this process would be guaranteed the salvation of their souls. As we hinted above, there were various systems of Gnostic thought, some of which persisted even within certain of the early Christian sects. Orthodox Christianity rejected Gnostic spirituality and theology from early on, but it could not ignore the existence of these 'rogue' forms of Christian observance.

This is clear in so many of the theological analyses of the New Testament writings. So the manner in which the writer of the Gospel according to John put together his narrative was at least partially determined by his efforts to refute the Gnostic heretics. Almost certainly, at times, the language of the Gnostics was embraced to repudiate the systems which they espoused. So, Ernst Käsemann, an influential commentator, writes:

> For John, all earthly tradition has a right to exist only if it serves the voice of Jesus, and it must be examined accordingly. If historically the gospel reflects the development which led from the enthusiasts of Corinth and of II Tim. (2.18) to Christian Gnosticisms, then its acceptance into the Church's canon took place through man's error and God's providence . . . However, the reception of the Fourth Gospel into the canon is but the most lucid and most significant example of the integration of originally opposing ideas and traditions into the ecclesiastical tradition.[9]

So the author of John's Gospel took on the Gnostics, even used their language, but ultimately rejected their theological system.

This is a particularly powerful description of the way in which the early Christian writers engaged with the culture in which they found themselves. Elsewhere another writer on the Johannine Gospel, Oscar Cullmann, makes a similar point:

> We have already seen that the Gospel of John as a whole has also been termed 'Gnostic'. This is correct in that the heterodox Judaism from which the Gospel derives displays *pre-Gnostic* features. This is why the Gospel was particularly valued in Gnostic circles.[10]

This is also why the Gospel of John was one of the latest of all the New Testament books (as we now describe them) to find its way into the canon throughout the early Christian Church. In some places it was not so accepted until well into the fourth century. Its language sounded Gnostic. Cullmann is careful thereafter to preserve the orthodoxy of the fourth Gospel, but this debate illustrates well the unavoidable requirement of the early Christian community to engage with the world in which it was set. Similar reflections can be made on the Pauline corpus too. Günther Bornkamm notes at one point:

> Amid the important discussions of the cross and wisdom in I Corinthians there is a passage which exposition even

today finds considerably more difficult than most (2:6–16). One of the main reasons is obvious: the apostle is drawing on the style of preaching favored by his 'Gnostic' opponents in Corinth and taking up a body of already current ideas; this he does, of course, as elsewhere, in order to amend both and give a different understanding of them.[11]

So it is clear that in the earliest Christian community, the Church's teaching was fashioned in response to, and by engaging with, the ambient culture. How did this evolve in the Patristic period? Certainly in the early second century similar reflections could be made to those already set out above. R. M. Grant, for example, comments on Ignatius of Antioch: 'Of all the Fathers of the second century, Ignatius probably came closest to Gnostic ways of thinking.'[12]

This sentence emerges towards the end of a thorough analysis of the relationship between Gnosticism and Christianity in the early centuries, which touches similar chords to our earlier reflections on the New Testament and which indeed refers back to that engagement itself.[13] A thorough and extended analysis of the development of the early Church would reveal a continuing tension between accommodation and counter-cultural trends. Part of this relates to a similar and related issue. This is the search for an 'original' and 'uncorrupted' faith. The nineteenth-century 'quest for the historical Jesus', touched upon in an earlier chapter, was one example of this search. Here German 'Liberal Protestants' were seeking to peel off the varnish of later cultural interpreters to reveal Jesus as he was when he walked the hills of Galilee. The question they were asking was: 'Who precisely was Jesus and what did he teach?' John Henry Newman's *Essay on the Development of Christian Doctrine* similarly assumed an original kernel of faith which later developed into the message as it had then been received within western catholic Christendom. The search for this original kernel once again assumes that the Christian gospel existed in a perfect form at a certain time and in a certain place. It existed in this form, it was believed, before it was later sullied by cultural accretions and accommodation. There is a real danger here, however, of trying to trap quicksilver in the hand. As soon as any message is proclaimed, any teaching offered, any text written, it is immediately and ineluctably thrust into the market place of hermeneutics or interpretation. Any two people sitting listening to the same speech will unavoidably come away with different slants, even if those slants vary imperceptibly.

This process was well described a generation ago by the scholar Robert Wilken. Early on in his analysis, Wilken speaks precisely to the issue we are addressing. Writing of the Patristic period, and notably of the time of Tertullian, he argues:

> The Christian construction of the past was taking shape in a world that prized antiquity, cherished tradition, and revered men of old. Christianity was a newcomer and could make no claim on antiquity. In the defense before the Greco-Roman world, Christian apologists, following a pattern set by Jewish apologists, tried to show that Christian truth was actually similar to the teachings of the philosophers and poets, and that Plato derived much of his doctrine from Moses.[14]

Here was cultural accommodation, then, aimed at making the Christian gospel understandable to a pagan world. Here were the beginnings of the art of Christian apologetics. This is arguably an art too little prized today, in a contemporary world which, often for quite different reasons from those of the first and second centuries, finds the Christian gospel and faith either opaque or idiorhythmic. Wilken traces this pattern of response through history, illustrating conflicts along the way. As this process continued, so there began to emerge a picture of an apostolic golden age. This was too the age to which Newman looked back. It was also the age that Pope Pius X and Cardinal Merry del Val tried to protect against the insidious incursions of the early twentieth-century Catholic Modernists. Wilken makes it clear, however, that this age was an illusory construction of later minds:

> The apostolic age is a creation of the Christian imagination. There never was a Golden Age when the Church was whole, perfect, pure-virginal. The faith was not purer, the Christians were not braver, the Church was not one and undivided.[15]

In what Wilken describes as the Eusebian view, the past, in the form of a particular understanding of the gospel rooted in the biblical, sub-apostolic and Patristic periods, assumes a definitive role which defines that understanding as the original gospel. This gospel is once again seen as that which is somehow unsullied by the encroachments or even the context of the ambient culture. Towards the end of his essay, Wilken opts for a more dynamic view of cultural engagement, quoting Gregory of Nyssa:

It is the same with one who fixes his gaze on the infinite beauty of God. It is constantly being discovered anew, and it is always seen as something new and strange in comparison with what the mind has already understood. And as God continues to reveal himself, man continues to wonder and he never exhausts his desire to see more, since what he is waiting for is always more magnificent, more divine, than all that he has already seen.[16]

So Wilken concludes: 'God is always being discovered anew. Men have seen his works in the past, but his fullness always lies ahead of us.'[17]

By definition this assumes a dynamic relationship of the Church and the Christian faith to history and contemporary culture. History is far from excluded; the past is essential in defining traditions (as Wilken argues) but it must be taken within the wider context of both the present and the future. The key issue, then, and one with which Richard Niebuhr famously engaged, is precisely in what manner this dynamic relationship operates. How can one achieve an effective engagement between gospel and culture without evacuating all distinctiveness within the Christian message? It is essential that an appropriate counter-culturism survives, but it cannot happen through a process within which the gospel is inoculated against the events and thought patterns of successive periods of history.

How does this discussion, then, relate to our main theme of the gospel touching the hearts of the English people and what is an appropriate or effective model to adopt? In this chapter we have so far argued that throughout history the Christian faith has perforce engaged with the culture within which it has found itself set. We looked briefly at just one tell-tale example in the New Testament text and we then extrapolated this approach forward into the following Christian centuries. Throughout the earlier part of those centuries the Christian faith engaged freshly within the surrounding pagan culture. Bede in his *Ecclesiastical*

History shows how Gregory the Great advises Augustine, as he sends him on his mission to the English. As he makes his way, so Augustine asks the Pope how he should handle the pagan religion that he encounters. Gregory favours a sensitive approach which engages with the surrounding culture while unashamedly proclaiming the new message of salvation in Jesus Christ. Such an approach was to be the foundation of Augustine's encounters with pagan temples and other places of worship.

> the temples of the idols among [the English] people should on no account be destroyed. The idols are to be destroyed, but the temples themselves are to be aspersed with holy water, altars set up in them and relics deposited there. For if these temples are well built, they must be purified from the worship of demons and dedicated to the service of the true God.[18]

The relationship between the new faith and its pagan predecessors varied from place to place, but undoubtedly there was a significant crossover. So, much of the emphasis on the miraculous related to a pantheistic pagan past. That past was one where the entire natural environment was endued with spirituality. In that world the isolating of the intervention of God from the laws of nature would have been unknown. Pagans thus embraced Christianity because they believed Christ to be a more powerful God than their own. This meant, of course, that part of that world of the miraculous was imported into Christianity, strengthening a strand that would have been there latent already. One can see the influence of that world very vividly in Bede's description of the miracles surrounding the missionary work of St Cuthbert. Similar accounts appear in many of the hagiographical works emanating from the seventh and eighth centuries, as England was re-evangelized during that period. Similar points could be made, of course, throughout Europe as Christianity and paganism found themselves in mutual engagement. Indeed, cynics will say that still, in those parts of Europe where a peasant culture survives, Christianity is a fairly thin overlay on a surviving pagan world. Often it has been in reaction to this that a more counter-cultural approach has been supported.

Nonetheless, the principles underlying this engagement have remained as the centuries rolled by. Effectively, what one identifies is a creative tension between those approaches which favour accommodation to culture and those which favour challenging the ambient culture at every point. Richard Niebuhr classically tackled this tension more than 50 years ago in his book *Christ and Culture*. Much of what he argues there stands, even if some of the detailed material has now been overtaken by further shifts in culture. He states the problem and then the aims of his book fairly early on:

> It is the purpose of the following chapter to set forth typical Christian answers to the problem of Christ and culture and so to contribute to the mutual understanding of variant and often conflicting Christian groups. The belief which lies back of this effort, however, is the conviction that Christ, as a living Lord, is answering the question in the totality of history and life in a fashion which transcends the wisdom of all his interpreters yet employs their partial insights and their necessary conflicts.[19]

In that brief extract, Niebuhr adverts to the way in which different Christian groups – and, by way of saying that, different theologians – have responded to the problem. If there is a tension then it is, of course, possible to relax that tension on either side of the argument. In a thorough analysis, Niebuhr then analyses the effects of relaxing the tension in either one direction or the other. This analysis is mirrored in his chapter titles: 'Christ against culture', indicates a full-blooded prophetic stance; 'The Christ of culture' implies an accommodating line; 'Christ above culture' suggests a certain level of disengagement and 'Christ and culture in paradox' speaks for itself.[20]

In his final two chapters, Niebuhr sets out his own creative work. Effectively he opts for a model where Christ is the 'transformer of culture'. This results from a positive response to the theological problem he has identified in his critique of the other approaches. Niebuhr roots this model in three theological convictions. First, creation is given an equally strong emphasis alongside redemption or atonement; it is possible for humanity to exercise an engaged response to the creative ordering work of God. Incarnation, then, stands with atonement, and humanity is given a place in God's activity in ordering the universe. To use Orthodox or predominantly eastern theological language, the human world may be capable of channelling the *divine energies*.

Humanity takes part in God's perichoresis: that is, in the total 'dance of creation'.

Then second, to avoid the dualism which is so often a danger, the model which Niebuhr explores sees human fallenness not as an absolute order of corruption. Instead *culture* is a corrupted order, a perversion of good. So, this culture must be converted and not overthrown. The fall is taken seriously but the influence of Irenaeus is there too; in other words, humanity is made in the image of God, but is being *transformed* into God's likeness.

Finally, the third underlying conviction relates to differing views of history. History is seen not as a series of violent conquests of one culture by another, although there are, of course, such moments of crisis. Instead there is a greater acceptance of synthesis between the divine and the contingent. There is a stronger eschatological and teleological element within Niebuhr's transformation model. Movement towards consummation through God's grace is a serious emphasis here. Culture unavoidably finds itself in a state of continuous change and it is moving towards a *telos* or goal in God. That *telos* embraces both good and evil. There is no final dualism. This is classically expressed in St John's passion narrative when, as Jesus dies and gives up the spirit, he cries out: 'It is finished' (John 19.30). There is a rich ambiguity here. The Greek word *tetelesthai* means both 'ending' and also 'accomplishment' and 'completion'. The evil within humanity that brings about the passion and death of Jesus is not ignored, but it is transformed within the one act of crucifixion into the accomplishment of God's purpose. John deliberately talks of Jesus being 'lifted up' on the cross. This lifting up has the double edge of transforming the cruelty of the crucifixion into the glorification of God in Jesus. This richness of language and theological emphasis is implied in Niebuhr's talk of the transformation of culture. Embracing the thought of F. D. Maurice, Niebuhr's notion of conversion is central.

Despite this sustained theological analysis, Niebuhr remains modest about his achievements and accepts that there must remain an element of the inconclusive in the relationship between gospel and culture. His final paragraph focuses his model and its implications very effectively. He writes:

To make our decisions in faith is to make them in view of the fact that no single man [sic] or group or historical time is the Church; but that there is a Church of faith in which we do our partial, relative work and on which we count. It is to make them in view of the fact that Christ is risen from the dead, and is not only the head of the Church but the redeemer of the world. It is to make them in view of the fact that the world of culture – man's achievement – exists within the world of grace – God's Kingdom.[21]

In these final chapters, as we respond to those critical moments in the life of the Church when the hearts of the people may have been lost, it is this transforming, converting view of culture which we shall embrace. Both Richard and Reinhold Niebuhr – and indeed, earlier on, in the nineteenth century, F. D. Maurice – stand within this tradition. It is not, however, a tradition that is universally endorsed and there are at least two clear strands of contemporary thought which need to be acknowledged which are stringently critical of such an approach. At the heart of their criticism lies a belief which is resonant with the work of Karl Barth. Throughout his life Barth, with varying degrees of vehemence, attacked the tradition of natural theology. This tradition assumes that human reason can reflect upon and contemplate the natural world – that is, every aspect of God's creation – and through this reflection arrive at certain systematic–dogmatic theological assertions about creation, providence and redemption. This stands behind the earlier 'proofs' for the existence of God. It also underpins Aristotelian approaches to Christian theology and most notably those which are dependent upon the thought of St Thomas Aquinas.

Barth's objection to such a theological method issues from his strong Augustinian emphasis on the fallenness of human nature. Our human nature has become so tainted that it is unthinkable that we should be able, through human reason, to reflect adequately upon God and divine providence. Our reason too is affected by our fallenness. This means that the starting point for theology must instead be *revelation* and specifically that means the person of Jesus Christ. Barth's commitment to revelation is not to a crude and fundamentalist view of Holy Scripture; that is not what he means by revelation. Instead, Barth's starting point is Christology, the Christian doctrine of Christ in terms of both Christ's *person* and Christ's *work*. Scripture is important but largely because of its witness to the person and work of Christ. The high doctrine of Christ which emerges would be sullied by any approach which relied upon human reason; engagement with culture is bound to be suspect.

In the past two decades, two significant theological strands have emerged which would endorse much of Barth's critique while beginning from rather different starting points. The more catholic of these is that school which has been styled Radical Orthodoxy. The Anglican theologian John Milbank has been the key exponent of this theological approach. Radical Orthodoxy is highly sophisticated, and in these pages we can neither do justice to it as a model nor offer an effective critique. Nonetheless, some passing reference is essential since we shall prescind from this sort of model very sharply. The aim of Radical Orthodoxy is to produce a radical critique of theology but this critique must begin with a similarly radical critique of secular philosophy.[22] There is, then, a deliberate standing apart from ambient culture; there is a strong emphasis on the redemptive work of Christ and thus, as with Barth, on Christology. The person and work of Jesus Christ challenges humanity. The theological matrices of Radical Orthodoxy, however, remain highly conceptual. As a model it deliberately stands apart from the surrounding culture so that Christ may act as both the key to a prophetic critique of society and also as the essential door into the Christian faith. Ultimately other secular philosophers do not have the capacity to offer a critique of the Christian faith; the only way into Christian faith is through an act of faith.[23] It is effectively about opting into a separate and hermetically sealed 'language game', to use a term coined by the linguistic philosopher Ludwig Wittgenstein.

Radical Orthodoxy, then, is a movement at whose heart is a profound rejection of any theological compromise with secularism. It rejects any dialogue with other 'creeds' or world-views and maintains that not only is the Christian interpretation unique, but it must be argued without any engagement with other movements of thought, theologies or philosophies. Interestingly enough, it rests its case on 'post-modern' foundations. That is, there is no metaphysic which can be used as the matrix on which to argue between different traditions. Each narrative is different and the Christian narrative, through revelation, that is its own story, unfolds the unique truth about the world and human existence. We can only understand this fully by participating in life in God. We do this classically in the Eucharist. Therefore there cannot be any engagement with contemporary society. Radical Orthodoxy assumes a purist Christian observance. As one critic has asked: 'If a Radical Orthodox theologian lay robbed, beaten and dying by the roadside, would he refuse the ministry and care of the Samaritan?' The rhetoric of this approach suggests he would.

This brief note should give some idea of the model espoused by Milbank and others. It has some similarities with Barth. It is, some would argue, a form of fideism: that is, one can only opt in through an act of faith, although the theological system itself remains highly sophisticated and dependent upon human reason in its logic. Third, it is almost supremely counter-cultural and would be keen to distance Christian theology from contemporary culture and prevalent secular philosophies. That indeed is, of course, its starting point. Can it really be an effective means of appealing once more to human hearts? Our answer here is in the negative. Its very isolation and complexity mean that it will not engage effectively with the needs and demands of contemporary society. Indeed, it is radically opposed to doing so. This moves us on to engage with a very different but equally combative and counter-cultural approach. This is the work of Stanley Hauerwas.

Hauerwas is an American Methodist (now Anglican) who has been influenced both by Karl Barth and also by the late Mennonite theologian John Howard Yoder. Hauerwas begins his critique with the Church itself. Christians are called to 'be the Church' and through that to live out the gospel of Jesus Christ. This he contrasts with twentieth-century theologians who have attempted to use the Christian gospel as a prophetic tool in a critical engagement in the world of national and international politics. One can see some clear parallels with Radical Orthodoxy. So, for similar reasons, Hauerwas is vehemently critical of the work of Reinhold Niebuhr.[24] Once again his disagreement lies in the area of Christology. He believes that Niebuhr's deliberate engagement with secular culture[25] is destructive of a truly prophetic and authentic Christology. In other words, the Church must simply 'be the Church' and live out the pattern of life encountered in Jesus Christ. This is its prophetic role. If people are converted by such prophetic living, then that is something for which to give thanks. If it is not effective in achieving such conversion, then the Church simply continues to live out its Christological imperative. It does so in the hope that people will eventually be convicted and converted by the Church living out the gospel in its life. To engage with the world and its politics can only disfigure the person of Christ as we are called to live out that person and God's work in him.

From this starting point, Hauerwas develops a virtue-based theology and theological ethics, structured by the life of the Church, and (but in a rather different manner) parallel to Radical Orthodoxy. The two dominical sacraments of Baptism and the Eucharist are at the centre. Through living this sacramental life, Christian people are formed individually and as a 'community of holiness' to live out the life to which Christ calls us. Hauerwas' approach is radically Christocentric. It is for this reason that he is critical of Reinhold Niebuhr and by dint of that also Paul Tillich. Hauerwas sees their Christological focus being blurred by their engagement and compromise with contemporary society. This, he argues, means that the essence of virtue encountered in Christ cannot form the character of individual Christians, and indeed that of the Church as it is called to be.

As is quite clear, this once again leads to both a counter-cultural and even a potentially isolationist model for Christian theology. Hauerwas himself makes this clear when he engages with secular philosophers, for whose work he shares an equal suspicion with the Radical Orthodox. So he writes, in true combative style:

> Theology is best done without apology. I therefore have no intention of apologising for the unapologetic character of this book. That I refuse to offer such an apology puts me at odds with a great deal of modern theology, which has adopted as its task to 'explain' – either to our cultural despisers or to what is a growing and more characteristic population, the indifferent – what Christians believe.[26]

Hauerwas, then, makes no bones about his counter-culturism. He is unapologetic for the unapologetic nature of his book. This is clear throughout his writings, but it is particularly interesting that in a number of cases Hauerwas is engaging with philosophers and theologians who are either avowedly, or at least implicitly, inhabiting territory not far distant from the homelands of Christian teaching and theology. So, for example, in responding to Iris Murdoch, who effectively was a Platonist with theistic sympathies while remaining an agnostic, Hauerwas writes at one point:

> In order not to keep you in suspense I will state my argument boldly. Murdoch's account of the moral life cannot be appropriated uncritically by Christian theologians for the simple reason that her understanding of the 'muddles' that constitute our lives is correlative to a metaphysics that we as Christians cannot accept. Christians believe that our lives are at once more captured by sin and yet sustained by a hope that, given Murdoch's account of the world, cannot help but appear false . . . Accordingly, Christians ask more of ourselves and our world than, I think, Murdoch can believe is warranted.[27]

The point that Hauerwas is making is, of course, perfectly cogent. There are very obviously places where the Christian gospel and other secular philosophies diverge. Nonetheless, the tendency through Hauerwas's combative engagement with other philosophers and theologians is to inscribe a circle around both the Church and the Christian faith which is so counter-cultural as to be isolationist. A circle is drawn which shuts others out. Often he is accused of providing a sectarian model; once again, there is almost an unconscious drift towards some form of fideism, where Christianity is protected by not engaging with the surrounding culture. Such protection, however, could ultimately place the Christian faith in an intellectually isolated position. Such a position of isolation may make it very difficult for the Church to locate the hearts of those outside. Some may be persuaded or converted by the transparency of Christian community life lived after the pattern of Jesus Christ. Others may instead be left either utterly untouched or repelled by a form of theological and moral self-righteousness.

Hauerwas's engagement with Iris Murdoch is fascinating inasmuch as, in a quite different set of essays, one encounters a

Christian theologian responding to Murdoch (and others with whom Hauerwas is in dialogue) and arriving at very different conclusions. Here we are referring to Fergus Kerr's engagement with seven theologians and philosophers. There is one clear point in common between Hauerwas' and Kerr's essays. Both acknowledge the considerable areas of overlap between certain secular philosophers and Christian theologians. They both acknowledge also the sense in which secular and Christian writers arrive at conclusions which include a certain objectivity to their thought and which imply at the very least a nod in the direction of theism. Indeed, Kerr gives his essay collection the subtitle *Versions of Transcending Humanity*. Kerr, however, is far more prone to 'circle people in' than is Hauerwas. He is clear that it would be confusing, patronizing and just plain untrue to assume that these secular philosophers are theists or even Christians *unconsciously*. Indeed, he has critical things to say here. He notes:

> Uncovering the theological conceptions at work in the projects of these philosophers, as well as sometimes clarifying what they are up to, often reveals the inadequacy of their assumptions about theology – Christian theology in all these cases ... It is chastening for theologians to discover how little many of their contemporaries, in what were related fields of study not so long ago, know about Christianity, and how deeply they sometimes misconceive it.[28]

When Kerr comes to review the works of Iris Murdoch, like Hauerwas he too points to significant divergences and differences. There is, however, an underlying sympathy. One brief quotation will illustrate the point. In his essay on Murdoch Kerr notes:

> To speak of 'religious language' as something specialised, supposedly expressive rather than referential, is to separate religion from the truth-seeking struggle of life as a whole: 'religion is not a special subject or one activity among others'. What is required is *attentiveness* – a learning, often with immense difficulty to wait for something to be revealed, to wait for illumination from something other than oneself.[29]

Here, then, is a clear embracing of insights from Iris Murdoch, a philosopher with a keen sense of the importance of contemplation, albeit starting from an agnostic or even apparently atheistic standpoint. Here is Kerr, coming from the Aristotelian tradition in theology, seeking places where transcendent theologies and philosophies may touch each other. Here too is a refusal to separate out the secular and religious: religion is not a special subject or one activity among others. Kerr's book is ultimately a testimony to the way in which such convergences have developed, often unconsciously and, as he notes, including a number of misconceptions about the worlds of discourse within which each individual philosopher's thought may be overlapping.

Now we are in a world where potentially others are 'circled in'. Admittedly at this point we are dealing at a level of considerable intellectual sophistication. Nonetheless the implications which come along with this may run far more deeply and widely. If cultural transformation and conversion is to be embraced then that needs to happen at all levels. Clearly in the combative discussions between theologians at present, there are implications about how Christianity should make its appeal to the hearts of all people. Hauerwas is unapologetic about opposing apologetics. Our argument is tending in the opposite direction to include both a theological apologetics and a real engagement with the life and politics of the world around us. It is interesting to note that Reinhold Niebuhr is one of the few theologians of the twentieth century to have had an impact upon the politics of both the United States of America and the UK. Tony Benn and Rab Butler showed gratitude for his writings, as indeed did John F. Kennedy. Often his influence was upon those who, in both countries, effectively espoused 'one-nation politics'.

It may be appropriate, then, to conclude this chapter with both brothers Niebuhr, Richard and Reinhold. The argument of Richard's typology of culture, despite his humility about its finality, makes possible – or, better, points to the foundations – on which his brother Reinhold had based both his foundational theology and consequently his social ethics. At one point, Richard argues:

> For the Christian the critical present decision of loyalty and disloyalty to Christ in the midst of his cultural tasks is always such a historical decision. He confronts a compresent, a contemporaneous Christ; but this Christ has a history, he is remembered and is expected.[30]

There is thus a clear dialectic to his thought. This is not a pure compromise with the values of the age – far from it. Furthermore, it was such an approach which led to Reinhold Niebuhr's social ethics. Often described as Christian *realism*, the dialectic sought by Reinhold Niebuhr was realistic about human fallenness yet idealistic about the image of God to which we are called, and as seen in the face of Christ. One of his better-known aphorisms captures this. He wrote in 1944, towards the end of the Second World War: 'Man's capacity for justice makes democracy possible; but man's inclination to injustice makes democracy necessary.'[31]

This encapsulates Niebuhr's approach to social ethics, which is also summed up in the prayer attributed to him:

God grant me the serenity
to accept the things I cannot change,
the courage to change the things I can,
and the wisdom to know the difference.[32]

This stood at the centre of his thinking about the capacity of *individuals* to move towards such aspirations and the impossibility of simply extrapolating that to *societies and human groups*.[33] Arguably it was Niebuhr's realism about human nature, combined with his Christological idealism, which enabled his theologically argued ethics to have such an impact upon politicians and statesmen on both sides of the Atlantic. Perhaps we have arrived at the place from which we started:

But love and I had the wit to win –
We drew a circle that took them in.[34]

8

Herding cats?

Macavity's a Mystery Cat: he's called the Hidden Paw –
For he's the master criminal who can defy the Law . . .

. . . Macavity, Macavity, there's no one like Macavity.
There never was a cat of such deceitfulness and suavity.
He always has an alibi, and one or two to spare:
At whatever time the deed took place –
MACAVITY WASN'T THERE.[1]

Part of the attractiveness of Eliot's *Old Possum's Book of Practical Cats* is the extraordinary variety of characters and of their individual personalities. It was this that made possible the genius of turning these poems into a stage play and a musical. Part of the fascination of the feline species is its ability to spawn both independence and individuality, combined with a capriciousness of spirit. If you are looking for loyalty and constancy you would not turn to a cat! Eliot demonstrates this further in another of his verses:

You have now learned enough to see
That cats are much like you and me
And other people whom we find
Possessed of various types of mind.[2]

As Eliot brings together Macavity, Gus, Old Deuteronomy, Mungo-jerrie, Rumpleteaser and all the rest, we see all too clearly how independent and different is each of these animals. Cats do not hunt in packs, and so arises the popular aphorism: 'It's like herding cats!' It is a vivid expression of frustration when something will just not come together, will not cohere. For cats of all animals are the most unherdable.

Many would now argue that to describe, to order and to govern a modern liberal democratic society is itself like an essay in herding cats. Western society seems to be moving almost exponentially towards an increasing fragmentation. The tide of individualism is apparently almost full. There seems to be an unstoppable process of human entropy: that is, a relentless energy towards increasing disorder. The 1960s cliché about 'doing one's own thing' seems to have arrived at some final fulfilment. Increasing deregulation of our world, both practically and morally, allows for each society, sub-culture, community and individual person to decide for themselves. This is the essence of what is called, in shorthand, 'post-modernism'! There can no longer be common values; personal autonomy is held to reign supreme.

Now this may be an exaggerated description of western society's present modus vivendi. John Grey makes an important point in his article on terrorism. He writes:

> The western intelligentsia as a whole is more confused and marginal than it has been for generations. In the Thirties, thinking people could reach for their Marx or Keynes in an effort to understand the present. During the cold war, they could pull John Dewey or Karl Popper down from the shelf. In the post-cold war period they flicked through the musty pages of Hayek in search of illumination. None of these thinkers has anything of interest to say about the circumstances we face today. All of them subscribed to the Enlightenment faith that as societies become more modern, they become more alike, accepting the same secular values and the same view of the world. That faith was always questionable. Today it is incredible.[3]

Tim Gorringe, indeed, refers ironically to another pressure of globalization leading to a new uniformity. Certainly there are different forces operating within the contemporary world.[4] After all, how could nations survive at all if this process did reach its final conclusion? There would be no common language nor agreed pattern of communication whatsoever. Even so, the recent rise in the tide of nationalism and of ethnic self-determination supports such a fragmentation theory. So, in the United Kingdom, devolution is a fact of life. The collapse of Yugoslavia led to the splintering of nations and to ethnic cleansing. Russia fears the collapse of the federation; this explains the brutal manner in which the Chechnyan revolution has been suppressed. It explains too Russia's covert politicking, and sabotage in former satellites

like Belarus, the Ukraine and Georgia. So, then, at one level fragmentation cannot be denied, even if some common values do
survive. Furthermore, often such fissiparation is supported or
catalysed through religion. Divisions between Christian and
Muslim societies are the most obvious example.

*

To where, then, in western culture should we trace the roots of
fragmentation? The popular answer to this question is often 'the
Enlightenment'. Eighteenth-century trends in thought are seen as
the source of these dramatic shifts. Influential as these shifts have
been, the roots of division go far deeper. Crucially they are spelt
out in Alasdair MacIntyre's classic analysis, to which we shall
return later. Indeed, the previous chapter alluded to fractures
in early Christianity. Differing attitudes towards exclusivity and
inclusivity within a particular Christian community imply the
existence of different groups with their own belief-systems and
projects. We encountered the various Gnostic movements with
which early Christianity found itself in dialogue or even in conflict. Throughout the early Christian centuries numerous groups
espoused very different beliefs which either were just held within
the Christian fold or were seen as heretical and driven outside
it. Augustine of Hippo, the pre-eminent theologian of the early
Christian west, began life as a Manichaean. Later he was arguing
against fragmentation within the Christian Church by opposing
the Donatist schism.

*

The existence of four different accounts of the life, ministry, passion and resurrection of Jesus, within the three synoptic Gospels
and then within the Johannine corpus, indicates different and,
at the very least, contrasting responses to Jesus and his part in
the history of human salvation. Then the witness of Paul is different again; it is still seen by some as a perversion of the gospel
of Jesus Christ. Orthodox Christianity has always denied this, but
there is no doubting the individuality of Paul's theological argument. So, in essence, difference and individuality both within the
Christian Church and within society more widely is part of the

essence of human existence. Indeed, such differences clearly pre-date Christianity. Although this may feel almost like simply stating a truism, it reminds us that the process of fracture and fragmentation is endemic within human communities and indeed within the Christian Church.

This makes all the more remarkable the growth of Christendom following the conversion of the Emperor Constantine in the early fourth century. Both the fact of Christendom itself and the establishment of the early ecumenical councils helped consolidate a burgeoning church and form it into a body that would be known as *catholic* or universal throughout both the eastern and western worlds of late antiquity. It would be tedious (and impossible within the compass of this present book) to chart the growth of Christendom alongside the numerous setbacks to its continued existence. Suffice to say that there would gradually emerge an increasing sense of a European Christian civilization, but that this emergence would be haphazard and swifter and more consistent in certain parts of the late antique and early mediaeval worlds, than in others.[5] Furthermore, some of the key components of this emergent order would surface far later on in the process. So, the significance of the growth of the monasteries and the subsequent emergence of a more developed sense of Christendom in the west can hardly be exaggerated. This did not take place until the twelfth century when the number of Benedictine foundations, in England alone, multiplied remarkably, going from about 30 at the beginning of the century to more than 300 by the year 1200.

The story of the growth of Christendom is, then, itself almost miraculous. Semi-political factors, including the conversion of Constantine, helped cement a growing unity not only of Christians but also of the temporal and spiritual life of Europe. Indeed, at times the two could hardly be separated. Augustine was to focus on this theme in his magnum opus, *The City of God*.[6] This book would set in train a continuing analysis of the ways of God's providence both through the Church and through the state over the next 1500 years. Nevertheless, alongside the emergence of Christendom, the inevitable process of fragmentation continued. In 1054, the eastern and western branches of Christendom fell into schism and thus set in train a divergence which would continue to deepen for almost 1000 years. The fractures in the papacy at the time of the Great Schism, in the fourteenth century, were another manifestation of the tendency towards division. It was, however, the Reformation that caused the most significant break of all.

Earlier on we visited the Reformation era in England and saw some of the effects of the changes in theology, spirituality and polity. Here, however, we need to touch on the wider ramifications of the Reformation. The effects of this division in Christendom can hardly be exaggerated and in many ways presage the ushering in of the modern world. These shifts are described with outstanding clarity and vividness by Diarmaid MacCulloch in his recent magisterial overview of the Reformation. In setting the context, MacCulloch points back to the cracks in the papacy made manifest in the Great Schism and the shift of the papacy from Rome to Avignon.[7] He then adverts to other cracks which begin to appear elsewhere and notably in England with the work of John Wyclif. In an apocalyptic passage MacCulloch writes:

> The biggest fear for western Christendom around 1500 was the prospect that it might disappear altogether. Except for Iceland and the barely populated far north of Scandinavia, none of its boundaries were stable or uncontested in 1500, and some were in retreat. At both extremes were decay and failure. Over the Atlantic Ocean in the north west, the Scandinavian colonies founded in Greenland in earlier centuries had finally died out, cut off from their homelands in Europe, the population malnourished, inbred and sick, and curiously unable to follow the strategies for survival of the nomadic Inuits who lived and flourished around them. To the south-east, the most surprising frontier of Latin Christianity lay in the Mediterranean Sea, six hundred miles further east than Greece: the major island of Cyprus, obstinate survivor from the western crusading exploits of the twelfth and thirteenth centuries.[8]

MacCulloch's engaging analysis sets out not only the historical setbacks of Christianity but more than that: within its wider compass, his book also uncovers the theological, spiritual and political shifts and fragmentations that were to be described by the term 'Reformation'. This was nothing less than a cultural earthquake. It was an earthquake the further tremors of which Christopher Dawson had outlined and warned of in an earlier generation. Dawson was clear that although the Reformation, its reverberations and its historical inheritance were facts of life, they were facts which had had far more severe effects upon European civilization than is often realized. Dawson looked back to the conversion of the Barbarian migrants and of the subsequent complex interrelationship which developed between Church and state with the extension of the Carolingian Empire. This, he argued, resulted in a Carolingian understanding of Christianity as a force for social unity. The Carolingian Empire became a society of Christian people.[9] Here are the beginnings of Christendom, but they were beginnings presaged earlier still in the various missionary journeys both from Rome and from Ireland in the sixth and seventh centuries. It was this remarkable and emerging unity which the Reformation would shatter for ever. Dawson is under no illusions about the effects of the Reformation, not simply upon Christianity but also on culture more widely and on the unfolding of politics and the growth of nation-states in modern Europe. So he writes:

> Of all divisions between Christians, that between Catholics and Protestants is the deepest and the most pregnant in its historical consequences ... The Catholic and Protestant worlds have been divided from one another by centuries of war and power politics, and the result has been that they no longer share a common social experience.[10]

Immediately he seeks to expand on the cultural effects of this and indeed of a later convergence:

> It was not until the nineteenth century that this state of cultural separation came to an end; and the change was especially sharp in the English-speaking countries when Catholicism and Protestantism finally came together within the same societies and cultures ... It is only in quite recent times that they have come to share a common culture. But this culture is a purely secular one; and one of the reasons that it is so completely secular is that there has been this complete cleavage of spiritual tradition and absence of intellectual contact between Catholics and Protestants.[11]

This reflection is interesting in the light of our earlier discussion of secularization. It may also explain some of the phenomena described by Owen Chadwick and adverted to earlier; the world has increasingly been described from two different and mutually exclusive points of view, the secular and the religious. It is one of the sources of the frequently quoted contemporary aphorism: 'I am not a religious person, but . . .' . Dawson is clear that the fragmentation issuing from the Reformation forms at least part of the root of so-called secularization, and notably what Chadwick calls 'the secularization of the European mind'.

Dawson is at pains to make it clear that there were, however, positive contributions from both Catholic and Protestant Christianity after the Reformation divide. So within Catholicism there was a return to moral discipline seen most clearly in the flowering of the Jesuits. There was also an interiorization and intensive cultivation of the spiritual life; this is seen in both the Lutheran pietistic movement and the work of the Spanish mystics. Then finally there was the benefiting of both Catholic and Protestant Europe from the new learning released by the Renaissance; Christian humanism was the most obvious fruit of this movement.[12]

Even so, however, some of these movements, and most notably that of the interiorization of the spiritual life, would leave an ambiguous legacy. Such interiorization led to a privatizing and individualizing of vocation and to the assumption that each Christian soul related most directly to God alone. It became the source of frequent claims in contemporary Christian spirituality of the sort: 'This is *my* vocation' or 'It is vital that I make *my* communion.' It was one of the ultimate sources, then, of the 'privatization' of religion. This phenomenon has had its impact both within and outside divided Christendom. Religion is now generally seen as a purely personal affair and conversation about religion is often deemed as embarrassing in the contemporary world. This point is made clear also by Grace Davie in her analysis of Christianity in contemporary European culture, when she notes the effects of sociological shifts upon Christian spirituality. These shifts combined with the differentiation of religion from the secular has also contributed to the 'stand-off' between the Christian Church and the world of politics. So, for example, at the publication of the report commissioned by the Archbishop of Canterbury, *Faith in the City*, in 1988, the report was dismissed by some as pure Marxist analysis. This reaction stands alongside a more general attitude that the Church and clergy should not involve themselves in politics. Many of these tendencies are hinted at by Christopher Dawson.

Dawson's analysis, then, contributes to our wider reflections on the fragmentation of Christendom. Indeed, he also follows up his historical critique of the Reformation by looking at the Counter-Reformation, Wesleyanism in North America, the Enlightenment and the French Revolution.

Further fragmentation did, of course, follow and certainly the eighteenth-century Enlightenment contributed to the collapse of any sense of united Christendom or Christian culture in Europe. Ironically, the nineteenth-century extensions of the Church into Africa and Asia would later, through cultural difference, also add to the increasing variety and fissiparation within the Christian order of things.

There is, however, an irony in all that we have said so far. It may well now feel like 'herding cats' as we seek to describe the fragmented scene which represents modern western culture. It is difficult to feel any sense of a unifying force within much of western society. This is felt very sharply by those responsible for leading the Church and by those who teach Christian theology, since the Christian gospel has hitherto been seen as the interpretative story par excellence for understanding European culture. Nevertheless, this fragmentation masks a far more remarkable reality. The unity from which this fragmentation marks a retreat was an extraordinary reality or achievement. The growth of a common European culture from Carolingian times, and possibly from even before that, runs against so much of our common human experience. The Old Testament myth of Babel describes a common feature of human life: a multiplicity of languages implies ever-increasing dislocation; cultures seem to be in a state of constant fragmentation and division. There is a parallel model for this in the world of science. Scientists tell us that the universe is continually progressing in the direction of an increasing disorder. This process has the technical name 'entropy'. Entropy is, by definition, always increasing. Putting things in this way is simply to offer a prose description of the Second Law of Thermodynamics. So the only way of reversing entropy is to pour in ever more energy. The building of Christendom, then, is in one sense a denial of cultural entropy. Somehow the spread of the Christian gospel, especially following the conversion of Constantine, led to a remarkably unified culture which could be recognized as 'one' despite the variety of its manifestations in different parts of Europe. It appears to have been the 'energy' of a Christian interpretation of society that reversed the all too frequently observed fragmentation of human civilization. Cultural entropy was reversed through the spirit of Christendom. The twelfth-century flowering of the Benedictine life consolidated and strengthened this remarkable flowering of a European culture.

Paradoxically, it could be argued that it was the unlocking of a still more primitively unchanged version of that same culture which would be one of the key contributors to the collapse of this unity. The fall of Constantinople, in 1453, was but the iconic moment in a shift which opened up the now separated worlds of eastern and western European Christian culture. Before 1054 these two worlds had at least theoretically been one, despite the growth of different cultural forms in the east and in the west. The opening up of Byzantine Christianity to the west at the end of the fifteenth century would open the gates to a new world, and a world which is effectively still unfolding.

*

That sense of 'unfolding' became clearer still towards the end of the seventeenth century and throughout the eighteenth century. What is now loosely known as the 'Enlightenment' began to open up in a variety of ways. The writings of the English empirical philosopher John Locke marked a firm emphasis upon human reason. Modern science was emerging at this same time, and was represented most obviously in England in the works of Sir Isaac Newton. Newton remained a firm believer, but the intervention of the Creator was now placed at a slightly greater distance. The rise of the deists, who believed in a non-interventionist God, was one sign of this. Joseph Addison's famous hymn is now sometimes still seen as the anthem of the deists. The final verse summarizes something of the deist's world or universe:

What though in solemn silence all
Move round the dark terrestrial ball;
What though nor real voice nor sound
Amid their radiant orbs be found;
In reason's ear they all rejoice,
And utter forth a glorious voice;
For ever singing as they shine,
'The hand that made us is divine . . .'

It was not that the deists had lost confidence in the Creator, but rather that they had lost confidence in the Creator's desire or ability to intervene in the universe that that same Creator had made. Those celestial orbs had been set in course but then left to continue rolling on in their chosen orbits.

Alexander Pope, himself a Catholic, had seen this intellectual and religious movement as a failure of nerve, and sought to address it in his great philosophical poem: 'The Essay on Man'. He is keen to show that the operation of the universe is the best possible mode of operation or, in the words of another Enlightenment philosopher, the German, Gottfried Leibniz: 'This is the best of all possible worlds.' Following the 1759 Lisbon earthquake, Voltaire, in his philosophical satire *Candide*, portrayed Dr Pangloss, his 'hero', as the foolishly optimistic philosopher who argued from the same standpoint as that of Leibniz. Pope, taking a not dissimilar stance, argued for the perfection of the whole universe. So he writes:

Lo, the poor Indian, whose untutored mind
Sees God in clouds, or hears him in the wind;
His soul proud science never taught to stray
Far as the solar walk, or Milky Way;
Yet simple Nature to his hope has given,
Behind the cloud-topped hill, a humbler heaven . . .

So it should be clear that:

All are but parts of one stupendous whole,
Whose body, Nature is, and God the soul.

The fragmenting of thought, then, represented by the deists and still more by sceptical scientists and philosophers, is still a unity. Our failure to appreciate this follows from the fact of our fallenness and the principle of free will. In a lyrical passage, Pope expresses this central Christian belief:

Know then thyself, presume not God to scan;
The proper study of mankind is man.
Placed on this isthmus of a middle state,
A being darkly wise, and rudely great;
With too much knowledge for the sceptic side,
With too much weakness for the stoic's pride,
He hangs between; in doubt to act or rest,
In doubt his mind or body to prefer,
Born to die, but reas'ning but to err;
Alike in ignorance, his reason such,
Whether he thinks too little, or too much . . .
. . . Created half to rise, and half to fall
Great Lord of all things, yet a prey to all;
Sole judge of truth, in endless error hurled;
The glory, jest and riddle of the world.[13]

Pope's heroic couplets offer the classical picture of man, or of humanity, to use contemporary parlance. It is humanity's flawed reason that makes it impossible for us to appreciate the essence of Nature (that is, of the universe) in its integrity. Whether we accept Pope's solution to the problem or not, he was one of the most perspicacious, in his day, to see how the former integrity of knowledge, philosophy and humanity's appreciation of God's providential ways with the creation was beginning to fragment and fall apart. Indeed, it could be argued that it has been the failure of the intellectual community, since the Enlightenment, to appreciate this disintegration that has led to much of the philosophical and theological relativism of the modern period.

In the last quarter of the twentieth century there began to spring up a greater appreciation of this widespread disintegration of the western philosophical tradition. We have already mentioned Iris Murdoch's reversion to a Platonic philosophical matrix. In her Gifford Lectures she developed this argument and her late philosophical magnum opus summarized her project in its title: *Metaphysics as a Guide to Morals*. Despite her inability to embrace theism, she was determined to rediscover an objectivity which would underpin moral philosophy. Indeed, she uses Anselm's *ontological argument* for the existence of God to give objectivity to her argument; ultimately, however, she believes that the ontological argument directs us towards 'the Good', to use the Platonic model, rather than God. She concludes her book thus:

Paul Tillich describes theology as a response to 'the totality of man's creative self-interpretation in a particular period'. We need a theology which can continue without God. Why not call such a reflection a form of moral philosophy? All right, so long as it treats of those matters of 'ultimate concern', our experience of the unconditioned and our continued sense of what is holy. Tillich refers us to Psalm 139. 'Whither shall I go from your spirit, whither shall I flee from thy presence? If I ascend into heaven thou art there, if I make my bed in hell, behold thou art there also. If I take the wings of the morning and dwell in the uttermost parts of the sea, even there shall thy hand lead me, and thy right hand shall hold me.'[14]

Of course, this question picks up immediately the ambiguity of Murdoch's position with regard to theism and belief. Nevertheless, it does also indicate her profound concern to root philosophical discourse in a metaphysic, so that it is rooted objectively and points to a reality beyond itself. This argument itself recognizes the fragmented and relativized state of philosophical discourse within the western intellectual tradition at present. However, undoubtedly the most significant and influential recognition of this fragmentation is that described by Alasdair MacIntyre in his *After Virtue*, published now almost a generation ago. Concluding with his call for us to discover a new St Benedict, perhaps the most crucial part of his analysis is his description of the fragmentation of western philosophy at the Enlightenment. MacIntyre states this early on in his analysis:

> What I am going to suggest is that the key episodes in the social history which transformed, fragmented, and, if my extreme view is correct, largely displaced morality – and so created the possibility of the emotivist self with its characteristic form of relationship and modes of utterance – were episodes in the history of philosophy . . .[15]

One of the crucial links here, then, is between social history (which is a central part of cultural history) and the history of philosophy. This forms an important link between our earlier argument in relation to European Christian culture and this present reflection on the collapse of a common philosophical or theological understanding or tradition. In the past, MacIntyre argues, philosophy constituted a central form of social activity. There is a clear contrast here with our present world. MacIntyre investigates, too, shifts in French Enlightenment culture and shows them to be different in kind from those changes in belief alighted upon by Christopher Dawson when he talked of the Reformation and the secularization of Protestantism. So MacIntyre continues his argument:

> It is only in the later seventeenth and eighteenth century, when this distinguishing of the moral from the theological, the legal and the aesthetic has become a received doctrine, that the project of an independent rational justification of morality becomes not merely the concern of individual thinkers, but central to Northern European culture. A central thesis of this book is that the breakdown of this project provided the historical background against which the predicaments of our own culture can become intelligible.[16]

MacIntyre's title *After Virtue* captures the focus of this. Virtue, he argues, is at the centre of Aristotle's moral thought and it was the collapse of confidence in Aristotelian philosophy that led into philosophical modernity which was then, by definition, living *after virtue*. MacIntyre coins the phrase 'classical morality' which he himself qualifies later in his argument.[17] This tradition, this classical morality, is not a narrow series of commentaries on the Aristotelian texts, but instead it is a tradition which is both dependent upon and also in dialogue with Aristotle. Early on in his discussion, MacIntyre describes graphically the result of the collapse of confidence in this approach. It is the character of Enlightenment and modernity that there is no longer a continuity or tradition which can be traced. Instead, each successive philosopher sees himself as a critic of that which preceded him. It is each philosopher's task effectively to discredit, or at the very least to expose, the weaknesses in the earlier argument and to offer something which may well be new or innovative and which will then carry conviction.

Some beliefs will be shared by the contributors to the Enlightenment project. They will agree largely on the character of morality and on what a rational justification of morality would need to be. Nevertheless, this is a change in character from the classical tradition. Any connection between the precepts of morality and the fact of human nature has already disappeared. Part of this shift returns us to the secularization of morality and this issue will reappear again later. With devastating clarity, MacIntyre moves through the 'Enlightenment project' indicating a process of setting up moral arguments which only stand to be put down by the next moral philosopher who enters on to the project. There is thus no sense of a cumulative tradition which replaces the continuity and dialogue of what is earlier described as the 'classical tradition' rooted in the virtues. So MacIntyre argues of Kant, Hume, Kierkegaard and Diderot:

> Thus all these writers share in the project of constructing valid arguments which will move from premises concerning human nature as they understand it to conclusions about the authority of moral rules and precepts. I want to argue that any project of this form was bound to fail, because of an eradicable discrepancy between their shared conception of moral rules and precepts on the one hand and what was shared despite much larger divergences in their conception of human nature on the other. Both conceptions have a history and their relationship can only be made intelligible in the light of that history.[18]

Towards the end of his book, MacIntyre makes one more fascinating observation:

> So it was right to see *Nietzsche* as in some sense the ultimate antagonist of the Aristotelian tradition. But it now turns out to be the case that in the end the Nietzschean stance is only one more facet of that very moral culture of which Nietzsche took himself to be an implacable critic. It is therefore after all the case that the crucial moral opposition is between liberal individualism in some version or other and the Aristotelian tradition in some version or other.[19]

Now it may seem that we have come a long way from our argument about the Church losing the hearts of the English people, but that distance is nothing like as great as it seems at first sight. We began with fragmentation. Then we saw the remarkable growth of a European Christian culture issuing from both

Christendom and then the growth of the Benedictine tradition. Thereafter, with the release of classical learning at the Renaissance and the subsequent dividing of Christendom during the European Reformation, that amazing unity of cultural strands began to unravel. Christopher Dawson describes this well, and Alasdair MacIntyre then fills out the picture with that philosophical fragmentation born of the collapse of the unifying Aristotelian tradition. Both Dawson and MacIntyre point to the secularizing tendencies focused again by Owen Chadwick.

Dawson points explicitly to the important part played in this by the dramatic and anarchic events of the French Revolution unfolding between 1789 and 1794.[20] Here, more drastically than anywhere before, in the practical and historical events of the revolution, morality was sundered from its objective roots, and notably from any roots earthed, nurtured and watered by the Christian faith. Conor Cruise O'Brien in his groundbreaking study of Edmund Burke makes the point very sharply.[21] During his political career, on almost every issue Burke had shown himself to be a liberal. This was true on Ireland (his homeland, of course), on India and on the treatment of the American colonies. It was his reaction to the revolution in France, however, that would make him become a hero for conservatives. Burke saw that in the tragic events which unfolded both in the revolution itself and then later in the Vendée, there was a change 'in kind' towards the roots of morality. The earlier classical European moral tradition had already begun to fragment and here, in the events of 1789 in Paris, the practical outflow of such a shift could be seen. Burke was in no doubt about the significance of this. In his *Thoughts on French Affairs* he writes:

> The present Revolution in France seems to me to be of quite another character and description; and to bear little resemblance or analogy to any of those which have been brought about in Europe upon principles merely political. *It is a Revolution of doctrine and theoretical dogma.* [Burke's italics] It has a much greater resemblance to those changes which have been made upon religious grounds, in which a spirit of proselytism makes an essential part.
>
> The last Revolution of doctrine and theory which has happened in Europe, is the Reformation. It is not for my

purpose to take any notice here of the merits of that Revolution, but to state only of its effects.[22]

Those effects, he notes, were international in their impact. Hence, although Burke contrasts the French Revolution most sharply with England's 'Glorious Revolution', he is clear of the universal impact of the events in France. It was this, indeed, which would lead to an apparent volte face (which was in fact not a volte face but a specific, even an idiorhythmic response to one particular set of events) on the French Revolution which appeared to drive Burke towards an uncharacteristic conservatism. The impact of the divorcing of morality from an objective source could not be underestimated. Burke continues:

> In the modern world, before this time, there has been no instance of this spirit of general political faction, separated from religion, pervading several countries, and forming a principle of union between the partisans in each. But the thing is not less in human nature.[23]

Both the fragmentation of the European philosophical tradition, then, and the events of the revolution in France, which would presage still more terrifying events in the twentieth century, have had their impact upon the English scene. Burke saw this even in the late eighteenth century. This contributed to that wider fragmentation that went on apace in the twentieth century. Writing in the first half of that century, well before the mood swings of the 1960s and the coining of the term 'post-modernism' in the dying decades of the twentieth century, Louis MacNeice wrote:

> World is crazier and more of it than we think,
> Incorrigibly plural. I peel and portion
> A tangerine and spit the pips and feel
> The drunkenness of things being various.[24]

This fragmentation has taken its toll in the efforts of the Christian Church to win back human hearts in England, and more widely in Western Europe. Despite the efforts of the Reformation, as Christopher Dawson indicates, common currents still developed across the continent and across nations. The tradition of Renaissance Christian humanism is just one strand to which we have alluded earlier. Something of that was lost in the Enlightenment project, through a process which Alasdair

MacIntyre has described so vividly. Does something of it survive? If it does, might this be one strand that could be rewoven into a stronger cord of Christian consciousness in contemporary society. George Steiner, an eloquent commentator on European culture, has been both pessimistic and then, on occasion, wistfully hopeful. At the end of his analysis of language and translation he noted in 1975:

> It [the Kabbalah] records the conjecture, no doubt heretical, that there shall come a day when translation is not only unnecessary but inconceivable. Words will rebel against man. They will shake off the servitude of meaning. They will 'become only themselves, and as dead stones in our mouths'. In either case, men and women will have been freed forever from the burden and the splendour of the ruin at Babel. But which, one wonders, will be the greater silence?[25]

Fifteen years later, Steiner wrote rather more optimistically. In setting out his thesis, he wrote:

> This essay . . . proposes that any coherent understanding of what language is and how language performs, that any coherent account of the capacity of human speech to communicate meaning and feeling is in the final analysis, underwritten by the assumption of God's presence.[26]

Similar hints and hopes emerge at the end of MacIntyre's *After Virtue*. The last line, famously notes: 'We are waiting not for a Godot, but for another – doubtless very different – St Benedict.'[27]

It is these hints together with reflection on our other discoveries that we shall need to bring together as we seek for positive responses to the apparent alienation of many people, whose hearts may have somehow been hardened against the Church, and not softened by God's grace as both the Old and New Testaments suggest they should be. Can we reverse some of the entropy which seems endemic to modern culture? Are there elements of discourse which transcend fragmentation? Is it conceivable that even cats can be herded in certain conditions?

9

Between two worlds or more?

———◆———

> Wandering between two worlds, one dead,
> The other powerless to be born,
> With nowhere yet to rest my head,
> Like these, on earth I wait forlorn.
> Their faith, my tears, the world deride;
> I come to shed them at their side.[1]

Matthew Arnold wrote these lines, which he called 'Stanzas from the Grande Chartreuse', as part of a longer narrative poem while on his honeymoon. They are enigmatic words with perhaps a deliberate ambiguity about them. These two worlds may be both the enclosed world of the Carthusian monks and the everyday world experienced by all. But they may also be the two worlds of faith and agnosticism, leaving the writer caught between, 'With nowhere yet to rest my head.' For it was also on his honeymoon that Arnold would write the more often quoted words of 'Dover Beach':

> The sea of faith
> Was once, too, at the full, and round earth's shore
> Lay like the folds of a bright girdle furl'd;
> But now I only hear
> Its melancholy, long, withdrawing roar ...[2]

'Dover Beach' spells out fairly explicitly Arnold's own scepticism and uncertainty. The lines with which we began, however, sound a rather more elusive note. 'Wandering between two worlds' suggests a broader set of cultural shifts which are clearly not resolved: 'I wait forlorn.'

Much of this book has explored not just two worlds, but perhaps a succession or even a kaleidoscope of worlds. Now it is time to gather up these varied strands and to begin to see just what the challenges are that they offer both to the Christian believer and to Christian theologians. Then our final chapter will seek to discover whether these different worlds offer challenges which can also lead to opportunities. But before we start gathering up those strands it may be instructive to reflect for a little longer upon the shifts between worlds and what these shifts might say to us. Throughout our discussion we have found literature (and often imaginative literature) to shed light upon the transformations or metamorphoses which have given birth to new worlds over at least the past five centuries. A further glance at one literary figure whom we have encountered before, albeit briefly, may help us in our broader analysis. That figure is Thomas Hardy. An extract from his novel *Tess of the D'Urbervilles* is our starting point. His narrative sets the scene:

> It is the threshing of the last wheat-rick at Flintcomb Ash Farm . . . They were busy 'unhaling' the rick, that is stripping off the thatch . . . Close under the eaves of the stack, and as yet barely visible, was the red tyrant that the women had come to serve – a timber framed construction, with straps and wheels appertaining – the threshing-machine which, whilst it was going, kept up a despotic demand upon the endurance of their muscles and nerves.

So the key actor, the demonic machine, is brought on to the stage by Hardy. But he describes not only its mechanical physique, but also its insistent character and its relationship with the other dramatis personae. Hardy still does not leave the scene at that. He continues:

> A little way off there was another indistinct figure; this one black, with a sustained hiss that spoke of strength very much in reserve. The long chimney running up beside an ash tree, and the warmth which radiated from the spot explained without the necessity of much daylight that here was the engine which was to act as the *primum mobile* of this little world. By the engine stood a dark motionless being, a sooty and grimy embodiment of tallness, in a sort of trance, with a heap of coals by his side: it was the engineman.[3]

This is Hardy at his most symbolic. Natural and unnatural stand side by side – ash tree and chimney – two vertical contrasts. Then the threshing machine is also an innovative and demonic incursion within the landscape of Wessex. The thick black smoke which has sooted over the engine-man is a dark cloud, colouring the skies over Hardy's native Dorset. The imagery suggested by his description of the threshing machine aims to capture a dramatic shift of which Hardy was a direct historical witness. The earlier agrarian revolution which had accompanied the industrial revolution gathered pace in the nineteenth century. Hardy lived through a period of unparalleled change in the English countryside. Once again he lived on the boundary between two worlds. He uses this great demonic war-horse of a contraption to indicate just how profound these changes were destined to be. Elsewhere in his novels he also effectively acknowledges the unavoidable energy for change. In *The Return of the Native* the doomed hero, Clym Yeobright, wastes his life cutting furze. Hardy is thus aware of the growing futility of these dying arts, but he is equally prescient about the negative impact that the new technology is likely to have.

For these reasons moral, scientific and intellectual change and a certain sort of capricious fatalism are all caught up together in Hardy's poetry and prose. Here in *Tess*, the threshing machine presages the reappearance of the demonic anti-hero, Alec D'Urberville. It presages too Tess's murder of D'Urberville himself. So the primaeval forces of evil are inextricably bound into the modern ways of the world. Even his language hints at this – the threshing machine's engine becomes the *primum mobile* of 'this little world'. And none of this can be disconnected from the theological assumptions which appear to underpin people's lives. When Angel Clare, Tess's hapless husband, returns to his parental home, where the atmosphere is one of strict Calvinism, the narrative notes of Clare's mother: 'Mrs Clare, who cared no more at that moment for the stains of heterodoxy which had caused all this separation than for the dust upon his clothes'.[4] Such heterodoxy – now ignored – was nothing more than her son having married a woman who had borne an illegitimate child!

Earlier we hinted at the sociological changes which caused Hardy to reflect so insistently upon the death of one world and the birth of another. In some ways these changes happened more gently in Dorset than in any other English county. This, then, reinforces the significance of the transformations that were taking place. Hardy was in no doubt about the likely effects of these changes upon attitudes to religion and morality. Although he was far from being a sociologist or anthropologist, Hardy's observance of these shifts shows a remarkable perceptiveness about the dramatic and wholesale changes which were happening to society right down to the very deepest levels. In his poetry, on a number of occasions this shift is reflected in a manner not dissimilar to the mood reflected in Matthew Arnold's 'Dover Beach'. So in his much loved Christmas reflection he writes:

> If someone said on Christmas Eve,
> 'Come; see the oxen kneel
>
> In the lonely barton by yonder coomb
> Our childhood used to know,'
> I should go with him in the gloom,
> Hoping it might be so.[5]

Similarly in 'The Darkling Thrush', he writes:

> So little cause for carolings
> Of such ecstatic sound
> Was written on terrestrial things
> Afar or nigh around,
> That I could think there trembled through
> His happy goodnight air
> Some blessed Hope, whereof he knew
> And I was unaware.[6]

Neither of these pieces is dismissive of belief. Indeed, the upper case for 'Hope' indicates a lingering sense of the transcendent. Nevertheless, both suggest that Hardy sees himself fixed to the hinge between an old and a new world, the full significance of which hinge he cannot yet fully comprehend. Much of what we have described thus far in this book relates to a series of such hinges and a series of such worlds. Often the shift is not necessarily or pre-eminently at the intellectual level. Frequently, instead, it will be sociological, demographic or economic shifts which have been significant. What precisely have these shifts been? Do they relate to each other? Finally, how do they have an impact upon the wider religious consciousness of English society over time? To use the technical term, what are the effects of these changes seen diachronically – that is, across time?

Are there any echoes of Hardy's speculations, then, within the rest of this book? Our first snapshot took us to Eamon Duffy's fascinating study of the parish of Morebath over a number of generations during the sixteenth century. It could be argued that the changes observed at the Reformation were of a reverse nature to those which occurred in the nineteenth century. For, at the Reformation, were these not changes instigated by the Church which would then have an impact upon society locally? After all, it was the discontinuation of the adoration of images in the parish church at Morebath which made the keeping of the flocks of sheep for St Loy or St Sidwell unnecessary. Was not this just a change in the pattern of popular piety? Were people not naturally moving on to new modes of prayer and worship? It was a simple shift in everyday spirituality. That, however, is of course more than a facile analysis. The Reformation itself was also ineluctably political. The changes which began to be implemented were the result of policies enacted by the Crown and then implemented by the hierarchy of the Church.

Indeed, in some ways this is in direct contrast with the nineteenth and twentieth centuries. There undoubtedly significant changes were bubbling up, if not in popular culture then certainly in high culture. But even in popular culture, shifts within society prompted by industrialization would also have their effect. In the sixteenth century, it has become clear following recent research, that many of the early elements of the Reformation issued not from dissatisfaction among the laity and subsequent shifts in popular piety, but instead from political demands beginning with government. So it was in the late 1530s, during the Henrician Reformation, that the first changes were felt. In Duffy's Morebath, the merging of flocks into one 'store' for Our Lady removed the sense of individual responsibility for the care of the images which had existed hitherto. There had, until that time, been a sense of personal commitment to the economics of the parish church. This meant that, within the wider community, relationships between what we would now call 'secular' life and 'religious' life were underpinned by a feeling that each individual in the community was a stakeholder.

Before these changes took place, it was virtually impossible to distinguish between the practical and the devotional, the commercial and the religious, economics and piety. All were integrally related to each other.

As the Reformation gathered momentum, as we have seen, both the devotional images themselves and the associated need to provide revenue for their upkeep were abolished. Therefore, because of this the corporate responsibility for the upkeep of the church, through the local agricultural cycle, disappeared. The significance of this can hardly be overplayed. Here lay the beginnings of those distinctions that we have encountered in contemporary society. When a young woman deliberately makes her way into church, lights a candle, scribbles a prayer on a card left out for that purpose and then spends ten minutes in silence before either the Paschal candle or before a pricket stand, it is difficult to understand that as anything but a profoundly religious act. Yet, on many occasions, when I have encountered an individual expressing their innermost feelings or intentions in that way, the person, in an almost apologetic way reflects: 'I had to come in and light a candle and pray; I just had to do it, and I'm not a religious person.'

At the heart of this lies a division in perception, between what people might believe to be the 'ordinary things of life' and those things which are distinctively religious. The pre-Reformation Church would not have understood this distinction. Now this is not a plea to reinstate the devotion to images as it was practised in the late fifteenth century. Nor is it an obscurantist call to associate religion with an agrarian world which is alien not only to city dwellers but even to those who would, in the twenty-first century, try to recapture a rural idyll through the culture of weekend second homes. Instead, these shifts indicate how some of the responses encountered now in relation to religion have roots which go back to the Reformation period itself. These changes were also linked in with different views of providence to those most widely held in the western world at the present time. The prayers for rain and fair weather in the Book of Common Prayer are the remnants of such a theology of God's providential dealings with his creation.

Interestingly, this has sparked off new debate in relation to the future of Christianity globally. Philip Jenkins argues, for example, that there will be a new form of Christendom and that it will be centred in the global south.[7] This new Christendom may well pick up some of these earlier, even pre-Reformation views on providence and patterns of divine intervention. He argues that this new southern Christendom will be enthusiastic, spontaneous, fundamentalist and with a strong emphasis upon the supernatural. An emphasis on the expulsion of 'evil spirits' and a real commitment to healing from this perspective will be part of this new pattern. Many critics have already arisen to challenge Jenkins' conclusions.[8] Some of them criticize him for his paucity of knowledge or paucity of emphasis upon Orthodoxy in Europe. Orthodoxy, it is argued, still bears many of the same trademarks as those which Jenkins predicts will dominate the new southern Christianity.[9] So there are elements of what many western theologians would describe as pre-Reformation Christianity alive and well in parts of eastern Europe and the former nations of the Soviet Union. In these places there would not be the western cultural division between the secular and the religious.

A general consensus, however, emerges that this is not a route along which the majority of European or indeed North American churches and theologians should or will proceed.[10] Sociological as well as theological analysis, as we have already made clear, suggests that Europe in particular has already travelled a long way down a very different road. This road is characterized by a pattern of 'believing without belonging' where a small core of people are left vicariously to respond to the faith which others declare themselves to retain to different degrees and in a variety of ways. This pattern of observance also accounts for the survival of an element of 'folk religion' which is often closely associated with rites of passage at the times of birth, marriage and death. This is much more than one world away from the devotions of pre-Reformation Morebath.

This, then, raises fascinating questions with regard to the revolution which Morebath, and indeed the rest of England, experienced throughout much of the sixteenth century and most especially within the Henrician and Edwardian Reformations. Elements of the split between the modern concept of 'religious' and 'secular' begin to open up through the drastic changes forced upon popular devotion at the very beginning of the Reformation. Different in type and in cause to later shifts they may be; they remain, however, foundational. At the Reformation, the Crown, through the Church, effectively drove a clear division between local agriculture, economics and piety in a manner which had not happened before. It would effect changes in what we would now describe as the sociological context. It would certainly have a direct impact upon issues relating to the sociology of religion. What causal patterns can be drawn, if any, between these changes and those of the more immediately modern period? For as we noted just moments ago, these changes are *more than one* world away from our contemporary religious scene.

*

Our second historical excursion took us through very different country. It took us through the Civil War battlefields of William Laud and Charles I, through the wilderness territory of the Commonwealth period, into the tightly ordered legislation of the Restoration period and then into the Glorious Revolution and a new climate of toleration. The extraordinary history of this period led to a greater self-consciousness in the established Church and eventually to rather more clearly drawn boundaries. The existence of Dissent and of recusant Roman Catholicism was bound to have such an effect. It was within this context that the beginnings of Methodism began to emerge. Again, none of this can be extracted straightforwardly from the sociological changes of the period. We saw, in this analysis, how Wesley directed his attention to the poor and how this had a particular effect upon the 'new poor', the industrial poor. Both the established Church and the passionate determination of the early Methodists made it almost predictable that there would be a schism.

The emergence of new dioceses within the Church of England was very late; the first new dioceses (Manchester and Ripon) were not established until the 1830s and 1840s. Although W. M. Jacob's study of the eighteenth-century Church of England suggests that 'secularization', as it later became known, had not yet bitten, nevertheless he does still point to a new growth of individualism, which, as we shall note later, would be another key influence in changing people's attitudes to religion. Unquestionably, significant cultural and demographic shifts were beginning to make their mark. Although the Church of England appears to have remained a 'communal Church' serving the whole population, even so cracks were opening up beneath the surface. The effects of the industrial revolution were changing the face of England, and England was, of course, the first place in the world where this phenomenon had occurred. This meant that in significant parts of England – West Yorkshire, East Anglia and the North East – Methodism made great progress. In Cornwall it effectively became the Establishment in terms of Christian faith.

Once again, an interaction between sociological factors and piety would have its effect on the ability of the churches in England to touch the hearts of the people of England. In retrospect, it might appear that the inability of emergent Methodism and the established Church of England to work together to form one integrity was one of the great missed opportunities for Christianity in England. Such analyses are unsustainable, since we are entering the impossible world of what 'might have been'. Indeed, it is probably wisest to take the late eighteenth and early nineteenth centuries together at this point in the analysis. The early nineteenth century offers a vivid picture of Methodism's growth and notably in the new pro-spering urban industrial centres within England. The Church of England did engage, but it was almost always significantly later on the scene.

The nineteenth century, however, brought with it other and different trends and tendencies. These included the spread of Enlightenment ideas from continental Europe and their growth in England, too, with the work of Sir Henry Brougham and the Society for the Diffusion of Useful Knowledge and the par-allel growth of Utilitarianism led by James Mill and Jeremy Bentham. Novelists and poets focused these changes with great perceptiveness. Hardy pointed to the changes wrought both by the industrial and agrarian revolutions and also through the spread of Enlightenment thinking. In many ways, Jude Fawley, hero of *Jude the Obscure*, is a model of the self-educated working-class man profoundly touched by Enlightenment prin-ciples. Hardy shares much of this himself but still retains some sense of an unmoved mover, albeit without any clear moral sense.

This is illustrated sharply in his poem recording the sinking of the *Titanic*, 'The Convergence of the Twain':

> No mortal eye could see
> The intimate welding of their later history,
> Or sign that they were bent
> By paths coincident
> On being anon twin halves of one August event
> Till the Spinner of the Years
> Said 'Now!' and each one hears,
> And consummation comes, and jars two hemispheres.[11]

Elsewhere, he strikes a similar but more wistful note in his reflection on some lazy insects as he writes in his study:

> A shaded lamp and a waving blind,
> And the beat of a clock from the distant floor:
> On this scene enter – winged, horned and spined –
> A longlegs, a moth and a dumbledore;
> While 'mid my page there idly stands
> A sleepy fly, that rubs its hands . . .
>
> Thus meet we five, in this still place,
> At this point in time, at this point in space.
> – My guests besmear my new-penned line,
> Or bang at the lamp and fall supine.
> 'God's humblest they!' I muse. Yet why?
> They know Earth-secrets that know not I.[12]

Hardy is aware, more than most, of the existence of two worlds. He is most interesting when he brings together the various shifts that are taking place at the same time. He is aware of industrialization and bothered about the irrevocable change that this will bring. He is aware of the changes in the moral mood of nineteenth-century England. He is much hurt himself by Victorian snobbery – notably in the Church of England. But he is aware, too, of a new free-thinking morality which is emerging and which he realizes relates somehow to the philosophical tremors which are part of the Enlightenment. He is also conscious of shifts in the theological and religious landscape. Perhaps most interesting of all is his ability to bring all these together in his novels and poetry. 'The Convergence of the Twain' thus refers not only to the collision of the *Titanic* with the iceberg, it symbolizes too the clash between the new science and technology and the natural world, supremely painted in Hardy's Wessex landscapes. So this convergence refers to a still deeper collision between this emergent free-thinking ethic and the traditional religion and morality in which Hardy himself was nurtured. That nurture came both from his family, focused on his father, an upstanding local yeoman builder, and also from the local school at Dorchester. Hardy knew that these two worlds were jarring against each other, but he could not finally quite discern the denouement of this momentous engagement, hence his inability to turn his back on religion entirely.

This is the same world described by Owen Chadwick in his book on the secularization of human consciousness in the nineteenth century.[13] Both Hardy and Chadwick, in different ways, focus much on that movement described above which emerges from the eighteenth and nineteenth centuries. The very toleration which is born in the late seventeenth and early eighteenth centuries allows for the emergence of a greater pluralism and individualism in society as a whole. We shall return to this later. How, if at all, then, does this relate to the early divisions between religion and the secular which are the products of the early Reformation? There are clearly some links. To begin with, as Christopher Dawson opined, the Reformation was the single most dramatic fragmentation in European culture in modern history. The unity of western catholic Christianity (which developed into Christendom) had been fractured. Here was the beginning of the pluralism which would follow and indeed increase. Here too, in essence, lay the birth for many of *choice* in religion. Although, during the early period, one's religion was decided by one's geographical place of birth, ultimately – and notably with the growth of toleration – this offered people personal autonomy in religious choice. Pluralism and individualism came together.

Another notable link is the growing sense of there being two separated spheres of experience, the religious and the secular. As capitalism became the driving force in Western Europe, so Morebath's sheep would, almost without notice, pass from religion to industry. The Devonshire flocks would become part of a developed and commercial world of farming. Classically today, it is identified within the tents of the Royal Norfolk, the East of England, Great Yorkshire and the other county shows. Commerce is now one of the indicators of the secular, even within agriculture. If religion has any part to play in such a world, it is exemplified now by a model of chaplaincy, where the priest is flown in from outside to 'service the industry', as modern parlance would have it. This was a development which moved on apace in the eighteenth and nineteenth centuries. At the same time religion became more religious! That is, religion has increasingly been seen as a separated activity within modern life. Here there appear to be some clear contrasts with the changes in the early Reformation. The collapse of the cult of images described earlier did not lead immediately into the collapse of popular religion. Indeed, even contemporary studies of the Reformation allow for the fact that England did undoubtedly become progressively more Protestant in its popular religious practice, as the process of reform continued and deepened.

Later on, rather different but equally interesting shifts emerge. So, for example, from the Elizabethan period into the Laudian there does seem to have been another notable drift, at least within some families, away from the approved Protestantism of the Crown. This Protestantism was at its most extreme during Edward VI's reign and was made more 'Establishment' during the reign of Elizabeth I.[14] Pauline Croft has shown, however, that at least in one family of courtiers, the Cecils, religion moved back again in a more 'catholic direction' within three generations.[15] Already there was beginning to grow up a feeling of choice. We have adverted above to the increasing sense of choice following the Toleration Act of 1689, and still more obviously with the Catholic Emancipation Act in 1829. Popular religion continues (and indeed W. M. Jacob argues, it *prospers* in the Church of England) and diversifies in the eighteenth and nineteenth centuries. The 1851 Religious Census makes clear how Christianity continued to flourish, although it also indicated that already the effects of industrialization and urbanization were beginning to take their toll of religious culture. So there is a tension here: Arnold Bennett in *Anna of the Five Towns* and even Hardy in *Tess* admit to the existence of religious revival. Matthew Arnold and Hardy, however, are equally well aware of the coming together of two worlds, the uncertain signals of advancing and withdrawing tides. As with the early sixteenth century, we are once again between two worlds (or *at least* two worlds) but they are not the same two contrasting worlds, even though there remain some resonant notes.

*

This takes us into the twentieth century and on to the next stage of the journey along which we have travelled. Fascinatingly, Hardy offers us one of the best signposts to the catastrophe of the Great War, which again set up a seismic fault-line, creating two contrasting worlds. By 1914 Hardy was an elderly Victorian gentleman, and he was, as we have seen, very much a Victorian. Nonetheless, Hardy wrote a small number of pungent poems on the First World War and we quoted 'In Time of "The Breaking of Nations"' earlier. Paul Fussell, in his classic study of the Great War, wrote of Hardy: 'From his imagination was available almost ready-made and certainly well *a priori* – a vision, an action, and a tone superbly suitable for rendering an event constituting an immense and unprecedented Satire of Circumstance.'[16]

Satire of Circumstance was the title of a collection of poems which Hardy wrote during this period. As Fussell hints, the tragic unfolding events played precisely to Hardy's strengths. The unavoidability of officers and men – that is, gentry, yeomanry and ordinary working people – working together, living together and dying together in the trenches touched precisely on Hardy's own sensitivities. This also had the effect of relativizing these differences. The English class system did not disappear at a stroke, but it was transformed beyond reversal.

The other Hardyean aspect of the Great War, however, is the overwhelming sense of tragedy, and the effects which this had on the consciousness of the newly mixing classes in the trenches. This has been most sharply and superbly focused in the literature – notably the poetry, but also the novels – which emerged from this period. Theology too was hit by a revolution because of the Great War. Karl Barth's entire rejection of natural theology – that is, of humanity's inability to reach out to God through the intellect – begins with the tragic events of the Great War. In the Battle of the Somme alone, in 1916, more than 1,200,000 men died in battle in appalling conditions. Barth was convinced by these tragedies that such was human fallenness that it was meaningless to reflect on divinity using our own experience of God's creation. Revealed theology was the only starting point, beginning with the Word in the person of Jesus Christ. We cannot rely, he argued, on human rationality.

There is no doubt that the Great War did act as a lens which would no longer allow the human race to understand religiously the world in the manner in which it had before the conflict began. Furthermore, the brief flourishing of Catholic Modernism, at the end of the nineteenth and the beginning of the twentieth centuries, had also suggested a real shift of worlds. Once again, as we saw, Hardy was 'on the case'. The Modernists helped focus, and indeed bring into the open within Roman Catholicism, some of the intellectual movements of the nineteenth century. The writings of John Henry Newman, who died a Roman Catholic, are part of this, but it also embraces the work of Charles Darwin and the emergent theology from Germany in both the late eighteenth and nineteenth centuries. Anglicans played a less significant part during this period, although Geoffrey Studdert-Kennedy was to contribute to new ways of understanding God's omnipotence. Studdert-Kennedy's own experience had led him to argue that God could no longer be understood by most people as the unmoved mover. Jürgen Moltmann, in his great study of the possibility of suffering in God, acknowledges a debt to Studdert-Kennedy.[17]

From this period, then, once again emerges a double-pronged shift. The first is a profound cultural shift. This is hinted at in the mixing across the classes in the trenches. It runs still further, however, to an increasing sense of cynicism about both human nature and talk of divine providence. This was compounded during the Second World War by the events of the Holocaust or Shoah which has itself given birth to an enormous literary flowering. A further complication has been the globalization which has led to the existence of multi-cultural societies in the old world as well as in the new. Alongside the increased feeling of scepticism, the emphasis on individualism and choice has moved on apace, as indeed has the sense of the 'religious' and the 'secular' being different worlds. The earlier theory of secularization established during the 1960s may now have been discredited. Religion has clearly shown its continued power to motivate, and sometimes in terrifying ways. Religion has not gone away, nor has it died. Nonetheless, a different sort of 'secularization' is undeniable. It has its roots in those Morebath flocks and their early steps along the path towards industrialization! Much more, however, it owes its roots to the relativization which began with the Enlightenment but which has been reinforced by the cultural shifts of the nineteenth and twentieth centuries detailed earlier on. The 'brave new world' now feels to be a cliché, and this is partly because we are now a number of worlds further on. Between which worlds do we now find ourselves?

*

The picture which has emerged in this series of historical, sociological and cultural reflections is of a variety of movements which are certainly not identical to each other. It is hard to see how that could be possible, remembering the vast historical spectrum through which we have moved. What has been resonant throughout these different periods is the sense that religion cannot somehow be isolated from its surrounding culture. Our introductory chapter illustrated this using the unique example of St Kilda. The very uniqueness of St Kilda means that one ought not to try to prove too much from it. Nevertheless, once again the phenomena we discovered there are resonant with the shifts in mood and culture we have identified elsewhere. They also capture another recurring theme, clear in both those chapters relating to inclusivity and the growth of pluralism in what is now often described as a post-modernist world. The worlds from which the New Testament writings emerged were themselves varied, and clearly the theologies which evolved from them were coloured by the differing surrounding cultures. So the general background of different Gnostic beliefs left its mark upon the New Testament witness without making the New Testament, the Gospels or the Pauline material a Gnostic collection. This makes the issue of *cultural accommodation* a key consideration. Indeed, this is the focus around which much theological controversy continues to rage at the present time.

This issue has become all the more complex in the light of the increasing fragmentation of western culture, as described in our previous chapter. The collapse of common narratives, presaged

in the events of the Reformation and further accelerated by
the Enlightenment, has led to an unprecedented pluralism and
individualism, each of which has had its own impact upon our
religious perceptions and cognition. This means that the division
between the *religious* and the *secular* is further heightened by
the sheer plethora of different possibilities. So, a recent commentator on the effects of this upon approaches to Christian
mission notes:

> like everything else in a consumer society, religion becomes a
> choice. The peculiar thing about pluralism is that it leads to
> relativisation. When more than one faith is recognised, all
> religions are being relativised, which again leads to secular-
> isation and indifference. Pluralism brings an increased supply,
> gives people a choice and thus stimulates 'sale'. Religion is
> no longer a matter of necessity, but about choice and pre-
> ference and seen in connection with choice of life style.[18]

Mortensen here brings into play another factor. For not only
has the Christian tradition fragmented since the Reformation,
and not only has the integrity of the western philosophical tradition disappeared, but the advent of pluralism on the canvas of
faith has its own impact. No longer are separate faiths largely
restricted to those places geographically known to be their traditional spheres of influence. Instead, globalization has led to
a kaleidoscope of faiths in many parts of the world, including
Western Europe and North America. The process of relativization to which Mortensen rightly adverts is extended by the avail-
ability of choice between different faiths.

These phenomena are assisted by the growth of individualism,
which we have already identified, and also by the influence of
certain elements of Enlightenment rationalism. Mortensen also
underlines the importance of these two tendencies:

> We usually draw a line from the Reformation, over the
> Enlightenment to modern times. The Reformation starts
> the development by questioning the authority of the
> Catholic Church. This is done by emphasising the indi-
> vidual, the 'pro me' of creation and salvation. What is the
> meaning of the Creation? It means that God created *me*
> [his italics] and all other creatures. This leads to an indi-

vidualism, which again questions our common basis for religious faith. In addition rationality takes its toll on the religious traditions.[19]

And so Mortensen notes:

> This is the beginning of the end of the sacred canopy, which had so far circumvented the societies. Individualism and reason are emphasised further by means of the Enlightenment. This leads to increased pluralism and secularisation.[20]

Further on, Mortensen allows his argument to become rather too sweeping and generalized in both its conclusions and their implications for Christianity globally and for Christian belief. Nonetheless, his summary of the effects of individualism and pluralism together is well focused. There is no doubt that we are living again between two or more worlds. Our conclusions in this chapter, then, have been that a variety of different cultural and religious shifts have, both individually and sometimes in resonance with each other, had an impact upon both communal and individual religious perception, cognition and practice. Many of these shifts have been common throughout western culture. The way they have had impact within England remains, however, specific. This specificity relates to empirical historical factors, often of political origin, within English culture. So the relationship of Roman Catholicism in England to other Christian churches (and most notably to the Church of England) has been fashioned by the specific political factors of the 'English reformations' in the sixteenth century. There is a greater self-consciousness within English Roman Catholicism, giving it a more sectarian edge. The origins here really were political as much as religious. The specificity of the English situation relates too to the manner in which the Church, and later the churches, in England responded to these changes. The Puritan Revolution, and the subsequent restoration of the monarchy, led to the unique manner in which first of all the state, and then later the different Christian churches and groups, adjusted and related to an emerging toleration. The unique contribution of John Wesley cannot be ignored here either. These two sets of factors have been key determinants of the ways in which the churches have lost or retained the hearts of the English people at different points in history.

It would be facile to argue that such responses led directly to decreases in the numbers practising the Christian faith and attending church at various points in history. W. M. Jacob has suggested, for example, that in the eighteenth century much of the population remained loyal to the Church of England.[21] Extrapolating directly from effects upon churchgoing in previous ages is to allow twentieth- and twenty-first-century preoccupations to influence cultural analysis.

It is clear, of course, that in Western Europe, and notably in England, the Christian faith has increasingly been practised vicariously by a minority on behalf of a majority. The factors outlined above may suggest some of the reasons for the shift in this direction. What lessons, then, if any, might we learn from this analysis? Moreover, might these lessons direct us towards a more effective response from the churches at the start of this third Christian millennium?

10

Reversing entropy

Someone inside me sketches a cross – askew,
A child's – on seeing that stick crossed with a stick,
Some simple ancestor, perhaps, that knew,
Centuries ago when all were Catholic,
That this archaic trick
Brings to the heart and the fingers what was done
One spring day in Judaea to Three in One;

When God and Man in more than love's embrace,
Far from their heaven and tumult died,
And the Holy Dove fluttered above that place
Seeking its desolate nest in the broken side,
And Nature cried
To see Heaven doff its glory to atone
For man, lest he should die in time, alone.[1]

Those two early stanzas from Edwin Muir's poem 'The Church'
gather together much of what we have encountered in these few
chapters. Most significantly of all, they point to an integration of
religion and the ordinary, and specifically of the Christian narrative. The first verse is poignant personally ever since my nine-year-
old son brought to me two slender pieces of broken branch,
childishly but firmly nailed together to form a cross. It was a
simple enough gift, but I have kept it ever since amid lots of
other debris in the shed where he made it. It turns out that both
he and his brother are now priests; who knows what divine pre-
science lay in this simple act? Whatever the answer might be to
that question, the young lad knew instinctively that God and the
ordinary are all of a piece. Undoubtedly the single most significant theme uncovered in these few snapshots is the separation of
religion from the everyday, within Western European culture.

As we have seen, this has happened in a variety of different
ways. At Morebath in the 1540s it was very obvious. The

Christian 'cult' no longer required local industry – in this case sheep farming – to support it. Much disappeared with this. The cult had changed. Religion and daily labour would each survive alone. With the rise of modern science and then Enlightenment thought, the religious and scientific–philosophical worlds began to breathe their own independent air. At the French Revolution, objectivity and morality rooted in the Christian faith were displaced by a galloping positivism which moved so fast between 1789 and 1794 that it became questionable as to whether any common morality would survive. Then urbanization divorced everyday life from the production of food and thus from dependence upon seasonal weather. Later the catastrophe of the Somme and Paaschendale raised questions as to whether there can be any real meaning in human existence. On one level this was a process almost of *dis-incarnation*. The confession of *God being present in humanity through Jesus Christ* and then, by extension, by grace in any human being, was being eroded. Oddly enough, it is easier now to engage twenty-first-century humanity in discussion about re-incarnation than it is about incarnation.

Yet, somewhere in his heart, that little boy nailing those two branches together had an instinct which in adulthood is apparently easily lost. The beginning and ending of that second stanza above may even be hinting at that. So it starts:

When God and Man in more than love's embrace

and it concludes:

For man, lest he should die in time, alone.

There are some magnificent contrasts and ambiguities there. To begin with, Man is reduced to lower case in that final line. What mechanisms are at work, then, in the crucifixion? Is this act itself an attempt to deny not only the perichoresis within the Holy Trinity, but also the coinherence of humanity and divinity implied in the Incarnation, which eastern theology has described as deification? Then in the last line too, what is the significance of the word 'alone'? Is it that man 'should die in time alone', that is, be shut out from the perspective of eternity? Or is it that man dies alone – cut off from God? Almost certainly it is both of these things, and indeed they too share their own coinherence. For God and eternity cannot be decoupled.

This, then, argues that at the heart of the Church's response to developing culture (and culture will perforce always be developing) must lie a tackling of this question. How can we prevent the young lady who had lit those candles, said those prayers and spent silent moments in God's presence, from protesting that she is not religious? The answer is, of course, not to re-indoctrinate her, but to try to understand how the gospel can again begin to engage with people's everyday experience. For a number of things come together to produce questioning and apparent negativity about religion. Hardy saw this with great percipience. He saw that sociological changes (as we should now call them), moral shifts and the development of religious thought ought all to be seen together. The threshing machine is not literally demonic, but it is one symbol of a series of changes which have transformed both contemporary society and also human consciousness and our sense of self-transcendence. Humanity is unique in its self-reflexive qualities, but there appears to have been an increasing fragmentation in the different ways in which that reflexivity operates. It is this that gives some of Hardy's personal portraits both their vivid and their frustrating character. Why is it that Tess and Angel cannot see their lives as a whole and take a grip on their circumstances? Eventually they almost do so, but it is too late. In each of Hardy's great tragedies – *Tess, Jude, The Woodlanders, Far From the Madding Crowd, The Mayor of Casterbridge* – similar themes surface. Time and again different forces swirl around the characters, but they seem incapable of focusing on their whole world and so are blown by these perverse and capricious winds. In his reference to the Catholic Modernists, Hardy saw that religion in its intellectual, social and spiritual manifestations was a key to this. Sadly, the Catholic hierarchy had thrown that key away, he believed. Perhaps this influenced the nature of his First World War poems.

If, then, this captures even part of the truth, and the moving apart of religion and the ordinary is central, then Hardy's preoccupations may give us a clue to a contemporary response. He was clear that at least three influences were essential in all this. These related to an intellectual dilemma, a social dilemma and a spiritual dilemma. Also present there, of course, is a 'pre-sociological' analysis. Interestingly enough, it is this analysis (and it is doubtless also very significant) with which Christian commentators easily become obsessed.[2] The arguments of the sociologists of the 1960s, from Brian Wilson onwards through to the work of Steve Bruce and Callum Brown, have dominated the foreground. It was one of those 1960s debunkers who very early on gave the lie to the sociological analysis as being primary and ultimately final. Peter Berger saw that both the analysis and the relativizing effects to which it gave birth were themselves provisional. The relativizers are relativized and religion speaks to an objectivity which transcends this.[3]

But let us return to those other three strands which Hardy held in tension. First was a concern for the intellectual depth of faith. It is well explained implicitly in *Jude* and much of the poetry, as we have seen. It is stated explicitly in the preface to *Late Lyrics and Earlier*, when he addresses the suppression of Catholic Modernism. This, then, directs us to a concern for rediscovering the truth and objectivity and thus a true confidence in God. Then there is Hardy's concern for the social aspects of Christianity. Undoubtedly he suffered from a deep feeling of insecurity issuing from his sense of social inferiority. This, however, was reinforced most strongly by the attitudes of snobbery within the established Church. There is no doubt that these attitudes had a far wider effect in helping to lose the hearts of the English people. How might the Church, then, rediscover a real concern for the poor? Finally, and his poetry manifests this most obviously, Hardy retained a real sense of mystery, of worship and prayer. This is often misunderstood by even Hardy's greatest biographers. Claire Tomalin's excellent recent life of Hardy assumes him to be simply a particular example of that growing minority of Victorian atheists.[4] This is a great oversimplification of Hardy's religious development.[5] Only a couple of years before he died, at the age of 88, in 1928, he still cycled from his house Max Gate to Evensong at Stinsford. How shall the Church rediscover the mystery?

Three key challenges, then, lay before us: the rediscovery of God and truth; the rediscovery of the poor; the rediscovery of the mystery. We shall engage with each in turn.

*

Rediscovering God and the truth

> I look at the church again, and yet again,
> And think of those who house together in Hell,
> Cooped by ingenious theological men
> Expert to track the sour and musty smell
> Of sins they know too well;
> Until grown proud, they crib in rusty bars
> The love that moves the sun and the other stars.[6]

Edwin Muir's reflections move him on to theology and to the ability of the Church and theologians somehow to trap 'The Incarnate One'[7] in a hermetically sealed and thus self-contained argument. Sometimes theologians even allow themselves to be trapped by their interlocutors. The importance of producing an adequate undergirding reasoning for theology should never be dismissed. Here lay the seeds of some of the key writings of the Patristic period, including Justin Martyr's *Apology*, Origen's *Contra Celsum* and Irenaeus' *Adversus Haereses*. This too was part of what St Anselm sought to teach when he wrote of 'faith seeking understanding'. But at times the very attractiveness of the arguments of others can so tantalize and engage the apologists that they are led down misleading paths, as we saw earlier. Dean Inge's epigram rings in our ears. Perhaps this path is most dangerous when we engage on the surface with the phenomena, instead of analysing the deeper causes and the theological issues to which these relate. It was effectively this failing which undermined some of the more profound analyses during the 1960s. It was this sort of mistake which Berger argued against at the end of that decade.

Berger, himself a sociologist, took to task those who too simplistically engaged with the analysis of trends in society which pointed to what he called 'the alleged demise of the supernatural'.[8] Elsewhere Berger used an illuminating image to describe this mistake. He suggested that it was 'rather like trying to push the bus within which one was sitting'. A similar point is made by Andrew Kirk in his critique of post-modernity. He notes:

> Post-modernity is a much greater challenge to its own stated sentiments. To use a graphic metaphor, it eats its own tail. Post-modern convictions are shot through with

unconditional affirmations that sound remarkably like truth claims. If, however, they are no more than a collection of self-generating linguistic signs and symbols without any correspondence to a real world, beyond some collective inventive imagination, the statements made have no meaning. As, presumably, they cannot refer to any objective state of affairs, they are, according to subjective taste, equally valid and invalid. Thus, post-modern allegations about the modern project are, according to its own assumptions, strictly speaking empty.[9]

In the same way Berger acknowledges the relativizing effects of the sociological analysis; indeed, historical research can have a similarly relativizing effect. We can see below the surface of the society within which we ourselves live. What we cannot do, however – and here there is a parallel to what Einstein had to say about relativity in science – is avoid those relativizing effects on us ourselves as observers. In Berger's own language, the relativizers are relativized. He writes:

> This most emphatically does *not* [his italics] mean a search for religious phenomena that will somehow manifest themselves as different from human projections . . . The theological decision will have to be that, 'in, with and under' the immense array of human projections, there are indicators of a reality that is truly 'other' and that the religious imagination of man ultimately reflects.[10]

To return to Muir's poetry, 'rusty bars should not be allowed to crib' that truly other love which moves the sun and the other stars. This leads Berger to postulate, towards the end of his analysis, 'signals of transcendence'. These are indicators of this 'other' which theists describe as the transcendent God. They are testified to also in the scriptural witnesses through powerful controlling images, including those of resurrection, creation, redemption, exodus and others.[11] One of Berger's experimental *signals* which might be compared to the great controlling scriptural images is that of 'ordering'. So he explains: 'A child wakes up in the night, perhaps from a bad dream, and finds himself surrounded by darkness, alone, beset by nameless threats.'

The mother, Berger argues, will take the child and cradle him in the timeless gesture of the Magna Mater who became our Madonna. She will turn on a lamp, perhaps, which will encircle the scene with a warm glow of reassuring light. She will speak or sing to the child, and the contents of this communication will invariably be the same – 'Don't be afraid – everything is in order, everything is all right.' If all goes well, the child will be reassured, his trust in reality recovered, and in this trust he will return to sleep.[12]

So in all this the mother's words are not cynical or superficial, but testify to a reality which is the source and origin of our being. Berger talks of the mother, at this moment, as being nothing less than the high priestess of the protective order!

Berger's analysis retains significance, since that high tide of relativism of the 1960s has not ebbed away. Instead, the currents that caused that high tide have come together to form different aspects of what is now described as post-modernism. This is an impossibly elusive concept and has been used by both conservatives and liberals alike. There are elements of post-modernism, for example, in the 'radical orthodox' theologies referred to in an earlier chapter. Here post-modernism is used to argue for the distinctiveness of the Christian narrative protected from the corrosions of the secular world. Elsewhere, however, post-modernism is used to celebrate the multi-variety of narratives in our modern world. Effectively it is a celebration of relativism. To use the jargon, we can no longer rely on a 'meta-narrative': that is, one overarching narrative, explanation or metaphysic which speaks of the reality of all things. Berger's analysis still argues against this post-modern thesis, as indeed do some of the other commentators with whom we have already engaged.

At the heart of this discussion, then, is the issue of choice, raised sharply in our last chapter. Viigo Mortensen, we saw, argues that in a consumer society religion becomes a choice and that this helps us to lose any sense of common discourse. This phenomenon goes back further than we might imagine. One curious but illuminating example of the beginnings of this lies in the rise of a new eclecticism in the Christian churches within nineteenth-century England. There were a number of factors leading to this eclecticism. Curiously, one of the triggers that made possible such an eclecticism and such choice was the invention of the bicycle. Now many villagers could jump on their bicycles and choose which church in which village they would attend. So, Anthony Russell writes:

> . . . perhaps it was the more widespread availability of the bicycle, with developments such as chain drive and pneumatic tyres in the 1890s and the addition of three-speed gears and gas lamps in the 1900s, which did more to change the life and outlook of many villagers. For the bicycle represented a major onslaught on the localism and containment of traditional village life and was swiftly reflected in the marriage registers, as marriages between couples who were from the same parish began to decline.[13]

Later he reflects:

> The Middle Ages (in the more traditional understandings of community) ended in many country villages, it has been suggested, with the invention of the bicycle.[14]

Here, then, is one example of how, within Christianity, choice began to arise. The advent of the motor car, and also of cheap and widespread public transport, increased these possibilities manifold. Thereafter the twentieth century saw numerous other developments, including radio and television and indeed all forms of mass media which made the existence of choice all the more obvious. The most recent development has been, of course, that of the World Wide Web and the myriad choice which that makes available. It is these later developments, together with human mobility, that have ushered in so-called globalization. This has further increased the sense of choice and pluralism in matters of faith by placing alongside each other both the great world religions and a multiplicity of new religious movements. All of this leads to an even greater sense of fragmentation. This, in itself, lends credibility to the post-modernist theory of the collapse of any single overarching narrative.

In an interesting reflection on the attacks on the New York World Trade Center in September 2001, Christopher Knight faces just these questions. Here, he argues, some would see post-modernity supplementing modernity. The forces of the phenomena of modernity make this possible. Perhaps his key sentences are these, which reflect on how social forces work against a unity of life:

While these forces may have taken several generations to take effect fully, there is now, as a result of their action, a widespread 'pluralization of social life worlds' which has led, among other things, to a 'privatisation of religion'. Different value systems are adopted for different parts of life, with little or no overlap between them. Thus, for example, modern people, even 'religious' ones, may be exemplary as far as private life is concerned but – without any sense of dissonance – ruthless in business matters and extremely limited in their social ethics.[15]

Many of those issues with which we have engaged come together here. Pluralization and choice stand ironically alongside a new isolation set within a privatized approach to faith. But also, that key division between religions and the ordinary, faith and the everyday, reappears. In response to this, Knight makes an interesting comment on possible implications of this for Christianity and Islam:

> In addition, pluralistic accounts of revelation have begun to enter the mainstream of our thinking in recent years, allowing us to expand older, more general pluralist understandings of the relationships between Christianity and other faiths. These two strands of thinking, in combination, would certainly allow us to learn from Islam through a sort of 'convergent pluralism', and not least in the development of a critique of our society.[16]

Interestingly enough, Knight himself makes a passing reference to Berger's work on transcendence, as well as using Berger's later sociological analysis. Each of these analyses, then, points beyond relativization, beyond a simplistic acceptance of 'post-modern theory' to a deeper convergence and transcendence. It was these sorts of convergence which we saw in the work of Fergus Kerr in an earlier chapter. It was indeed also to such an ultimate objectivity that the philosophical analyses of both Alasdair MacIntyre and Iris Murdoch were pointing in their work. Hauerwas too, albeit using a different starting point for his theology and ecclesiology, argues for a renewed confidence in God and in the Christian tradition. Hauerwas is highly influenced by Karl Barth's strong insistence on the priority of revelation in the person of

Jesus Christ; our doctrine of Christ, he argues, must not be compromised. He is equally influenced by the Mennonite theologian John Howard Yoder; it is Yoder who lends to Hauerwas' analysis both its pacifist and its sectarian (Hauerwas would call it ecclesial) bias.

First, then, in responding to the loss of human hearts, the Christian Church needs to reclaim an appropriate confidence in the God of our Lord Jesus Christ. There are now a variety of different starting points for this, not all of which are mutually compatible. Nonetheless it is interesting to see some convergence in a desire to recover an overarching narrative, an objectivity in talk of truth, as the foundation for both theology and morals. This is a convergence which drives us back to a church and a theology which first and foremost focuses upon 'the love that moves the sun and the other stars'. That is at the heart of that stanza from Edwin Muir; that is where Dante ends his *Paradiso*; that is the key foundation for our response now. It is a response which must be anchored in a concern for God's world, in an undying attention to the vision of God and in speaking directly to the ordinary experience in people's lives.

So what does this say to the Church? A brief vignette may lead us towards an answer. In early December each year, Wakefield Cathedral, in West Yorkshire, hosts two services on a Sunday afternoon. They focus upon a Tree of Lights. A very large Christmas tree is bedecked with hundreds of tiny lights. These services, which are paralleled in many towns and cities across England, aim to minister to the thousands who have lost loved ones in the past year or years. The lights represent the 'light of Christ' pointing to the resurrection hope for those who have died. The service makes no attempt to offer a facile answer to the questions posed by death and bereavement; that would be to take advantage of those gathered there – it would also be hopelessly ineffective for most people.

Instead, the service acknowledges the brutal fact that 'in the midst of life we are in death'. It offers people an opportunity to grieve and it offers them too the chance to reflect, at least for an hour, upon death and the way in which it deepens the seriousness with which we understand our life. Not by accident, it does this in the context of a corporate act of worship. So people's undeniable dependence upon each other, under God, is recognized; it is also recognized in the context of worship. Even more significantly, our dependence upon God is recognized. So this restores to people's experience the opportunity to worship; it also demonstrates that worship is something which Christian faith and therefore the Church uniquely offers. Worship is an aspect of human experience engaged within by no other agency, organization or association. Most remarkable of all, the cathedral is packed twice over and might be filled more times still were that logistically possible.

Here, then, is the Church speaking vividly of the truths of God and relating them directly to the experience of people in their daily lives. It does so within an undeniably contemporary context. But here there are no compromised glances in the direction of God. The message of engagement with an objective transcendent God, despite the tragedies and ambiguities of death, is unmistakable.

This is not, however, a unique engagement. Churches within England have taken other related initiatives. So, Road Peace Services offer something similar for those who have lost loved ones in traffic accidents. In some places, too, a parish church will offer a service for all those whose funerals it has conducted in the past year or years. Other churches offer something similar to those who have brought children to baptism or who have been married. In each case the Church of God is re-establishing an obvious link with elemental aspects of our ordinary lives. Part of this process relates to 'rites of passage' at defined moments within the course of our lives. It hardly needs spelling out that this is a principle that could be extended very significantly. Other parts of our lives might equally be honoured and other experiences acknowledged, and this need not happen only within special services once a year. How can we engage weekly in our liturgy with those things which underpin our existence and which also speak of everyday highs, lows and even ordinariness?

This, then, is a practical challenge for the Church – to present the truths of human existence in the context of our belief in a loving Creator and Sustainer. But this has still more to teach the Church, for it implies an *apologetic* framework to our theological reflection. During and after the Second World War, in his writings and through radio broadcasts, C. S. Lewis offered Christian apologetic reflection upon people's experience. The problem of pain, questions of time and eternity, the nature of prayer – all were explored in an accessible fashion. Such reflection even underpinned the formative structure of the Narnia stories. Lewis' friend Austin Farrer did something similar through his preaching and, at a more 'high-brow' level, through his theological writings. Lewis' work may feel dated now, but the principles within which it is rooted remain essential. From time to time, since then, others have attempted helpful apologetic.[17] Such an apologetic method, both in worship and in the written word, is an essential way of *rediscovering God and truth* in our world. It is a challenge to the Church to rediscover this tradition in all its richness.

Such an approach to theological reflection has a long pedigree reaching back effectively to Paul's remarkable dialogue with his Jewish inheritance in his letter to the Romans. Justin Martyr continued this in his *Apology* in the second century, and Origen's *Contra Celsum*, to which we referred earlier, engages in a similar exercise. In the modern period, Schleiermacher's *Religion: Speeches to Its Cultured Despisers*, written at the very end of the eighteenth century, is a similar exercise in Christian apologetics. It is a method of theologizing which may be virtually *de rigueur* in a society where there are such strong secularizing and pluralizing gales blowing over the Christian doctrinal deposit. This requires both the Church and the wider theological community to be prepared to release itself from single-minded dogmatics and systematics, and instead to engage with questions of meaning and existence as they face people in their own lives. This is part of an essential re-engagement of religion with everyday life. What other challenges still remain?

Rediscovering the poor

I think of the Church, that stretched magnificence
Housing the crib, the desert, and the tree,
And the good Lord who lived on poverty's pence
Among the fishermen of Galilee,
Courting mortality,
And schooled himself to learn his human part:
A poor man schooled in didactic art.[18]

Throughout this book we have been attempting to reflect upon whether the *churches* in England lost the hearts of the people of

England and if so at which points and how. So our focus has not been purely upon the Church of England. Nonetheless, as the 'national church', the Church of England has often boasted of having a ministry to all who live in the land apart from those who have deliberately opted out by dint of no faith, other faith or other Christian observance. But has the Church of England ever been the church of the poor? All the evidence suggests that the Church of England has exercised a very broad ministry over the centuries; this was adverted in our quotation from W. M. Jacob in an earlier chapter where he was writing about the Church in the eighteenth century. Thomas Hardy, however, points to a gap, which appears to have opened up in the nineteenth century between the Church of England and the poor, certainly in rural areas. This drift seems to have become significant during the industrial revolution. We have already noted Methodism's focus upon and effectiveness with the poor, during its early history. We have also noted how late on the scene the Church of England was in building churches in the newly industrialized parts of England. Still, if one ministers in industrial or post-industrial England, there is frequently a sense that the Church of England has been the church of the 'gaffers' – that is, of the mill owners, the colliery entrepreneurs and the like.

But the Church of England is not unique in allowing itself to lose sight of the poor. The temporal power assumed by the papacy and by bishops more widely within the Middle Ages could too easily identify the Church with the authority of the ruling élites. Muir's stanza above makes the contrast well between a compromised Church and an authentic Church anchored in the roots of the gospel. He does so with his reference to Christ living 'on poverty's pence'. Later on in the poem, Muir paints his vision of the Church as it should be:

> Yet fortune to the new church, and may its door
> Never be shut, or yawn in empty state
> To daunt the poor in spirit, the always poor.[19]

There is no doubt of the authenticity of the Church's primary mission to the poor.[20] It is clear from the Gospel narratives both of Jesus and of his instructions to his own followers; so, for example: 'Go your way; behold I send you out as lambs in the midst of wolves. Carry no purse, no bag, no sandals.'[21] And then later: 'Sell your possessions, and give alms; provide yourselves with purses that do not grow old, with a treasure in the heavens that does not fail.'[22]

It was presumably St Francis of Assisi's embracing these comments literally that led to the remarkable flowering of the Friars Minor and indeed the Franciscan Third Order, even during his own lifetime. Francis believed himself called to 'rebuild Christ's Church' and this entailed, as a primary imperative, a mission to the poor. This is a mission which has been renewed frequently down the ages. Just a few recent examples may suffice. In the 1920s and 1930s the depression brought huge levels of unemployment and suffering to many. It was this that convicted Brother Douglas SSF to found what would eventually become the Society of St Francis, working with 'wayfarers' and other victims of the depression. So too, in the same period, was established 'The Brotherhood of the Way'. This again had a Franciscan ethos. The brethren wore civilian dress, no habit, but they too preached widely and worked with the poor; they lived on a shilling a day (now five pence!) spending the nights sleeping in church porches, bus shelters and the like.

Or, and largely within the Roman Catholic Church, there is the work of the Comunità da Sant' Egidio. Following the Second Vatican Council, and with the support of Pope Paul VI, Dr Andrea Riccardi and a number of colleagues set up the Community. It is a lay community where each member is committed to daily corporate prayer and also to work for the poor and outcast in the world. Beginning in Rome, it has now some 45,000 members worldwide. In Rome it runs, among other things: a residential home for children born with AIDS; a language school for impoverished immigrants; a soup kitchen for that same group of people; and food parcels which are taken to those living rough. Alongside this work locally, which is paralleled in its communities across the world, the community has also engaged in work of a more international nature. The peace agreement in Mozambique was brokered using the Comunità da Sant' Egidio, and there continues to be an annual international and ecumenical gathering focused upon prayers for peace. The papal gathering of religious leaders from across the world faiths in Assisi in 1986, hosted by Pope John Paul II, was orchestrated by the Community. The Community sees its task as living out the gospel and never allowing prayer and work for the poor to become divorced from each other. Perhaps most remarkable of all is that highly qualified, professional people give up much of their free time, often up to five half-days a week, in working for the poor.

Two other examples may fill out this part of our argument a little further. In 1983 the Bishop of Liverpool, David Sheppard, published his book *Bias to the Poor*.[23] In a lifetime of Christian ministry, including 11 years in one of the poorest parts of east London, Sheppard produced a manifesto for bringing Christian care for the poor and the underprivileged to the heart of the Church's witness. Sheppard himself lived out that vision and was not frightened of unpopularity when he took stances that ran counter to prevailing fashions either in the Church or in politics. Then, some 11 years later, was published *Faith in the City*,[24] commissioned by Robert Runcie, then Archbishop of Canterbury, following the spate of urban riots in Britain in the early 1980s. One of the most serious riots had erupted in Brixton, in south London, just two miles down the road from the Archbishop's official residence at Lambeth Palace. *Faith in the City* was a rigorous sociological and theological analysis of the state of English cities, with a particular focus on what the report called 'urban priority areas'. The report was addressed to both government and Church. It would be no exaggeration to say that of all reports produced by non-governmental organizations during the second half of the twentieth century, *Faith in the City* had more impact on the then Conservative government and on its New Labour successor than any other report. Its impact continues to be felt now, and the Church Urban Fund, established in the wake of the report, has distributed more than £30 million to church-based and other social projects over the past 20 years.

The significance of these different initiatives has been enormous, and returns the churches in England to the heart of the gospel. Often the churches appear to be caught in a time-warp, woven by an agenda largely set by the media. On his appointment, almost every new Anglican bishop is asked two questions without fail. They focus on homosexuality and the priesthood, and the ordination of women. By putting the poor back at the heart of the Church's witness, this time-warp can be unravelled and these other two issues not dismissed but set within the wider context of the untold suffering of poor and underprivileged people in Britain, in North America (where the problem is growing) and throughout the world.

For all his own insecurity, Thomas Hardy was accurate in pinpointing the Church of England's snobbery and failure to speak for the poor in the nineteenth century. Of course, there were exceptions, but the balance had slipped badly and this was highlighted by the events of the First World War. Alan Wilkinson has shown how many Church of England chaplains were unclear of their role and out of their depth throughout the conflict.[25] There were exceptions, and in these cases chaplains often found their theology, and even their concept of God, being transformed through their experience of the conflict. Again, the Great War had an enduring effect upon culture and class both within the Church of England and well beyond during the rest of the twentieth century. Studdert-Kennedy, Dick Sheppard (both outsiders in different ways) and others would return with a clear conviction to work for the poor. Later in the twentieth century another outsider, R. S. Thomas, Welsh priest and poet, wrote these lines:

> It's a long way off but inside it
> There are quite different things going on:
> Festivals at which the poor man
> Is king and the consumptive is
> Healed; mirrors in which the blind look
> At themselves and love looks at them
> Back; and industry is for mending
> The bent bones and the minds fractured
> By life. It's a long way off but to get
> There takes no time and admission
> Is free, if you will purge yourself
> Of desire, and present yourself with
> Your need only and the simple offering
> Of your faith, green as a leaf.[26]

Thomas encapsulates much of what our response might be if we are to engage once again within the hearts of all people. There is an easy assumption that the engagement of the Church with social issues results in an agency that loses sight of the Godward dimension; the Church becomes just one more welfare agency. The tradition of social engagement and critique, and the doctrine of the 'common good' within Roman Catholic social ethics, suggests precisely the opposite. Starting from Pope Leo XIII's encyclical *Rerum novarum* in 1891, there has been a succession of papal documents and other contributions from lay theologians, including Jacques Maritain and John Courtney Murray. All this work (and there are equally significant examples from the non-Catholic world, notably Reinhold Niebuhr and John Howard Yoder), this social and ethical teaching has been integrated into the life of worship and prayer. It is there too in the final line of Thomas' poem, bringing us back to that faith from which every response to the gospel springs.

One practical example of the need to retain a bias to the poor has manifested itself recently in South Yorkshire. The community of Lundwood comprises the north-eastern corner of the town of Barnsley. In the last quarter of the twentieth century, this community had been hit severely by the collapse of deep mining for coal in this part of England. The collieries around Barnsley have now all closed. The effects upon the *spirit* of the community did not leave the churches untouched. Both the Methodists and Roman Catholics were forced to close their churches. The Church of England retrenched by leaving the church there, but by attaching it to the next-door parish. This left the community without a resident priest. It also put an intolerable load upon the priest in the next-door parish, who already had a cure of some 12,000 souls.

In 2003 a decision was taken by the local Anglican diocese to put a priest back into Lundwood. A courageous young American accepted the challenge. Almost immediately after the decision was taken to put a priest back into the parish, the diocese was approached by a television production company. The company aimed to film two or three programmes in a Church of England parish where a new priest had been recently inducted, to see what the impact of that new priest's ministry might be. Lundwood was one of four possible locations and it was eventually selected to be the focus of these programmes. The television programme company, along with the Jerusalem Trust, put some money into the campaign to strengthen Christian witness there, although most of the television budget was spent on the programme production itself.[27] In the event, this investment of the Church in a new priest has had a very significant impact on this poor community. In the contemporary context, the television programmes have also, of course, had their impact on local patterns of religious observance.

This initiative did not stand alone. The local authority in Barnsley had already begun a significant programme for economic and social regeneration throughout the borough, including Lundwood. Furthermore, the ancient site of the Benedictine monastery of Monk Bretton, well within the boundaries of Lundwood parish, was singled out for development and use by the local community. Again the Church of England took the lead, and development of this site is now well underway for use educationally and for other community activities. None of this, of course, happens without financial investment and this has a clear impact upon the church and diocese. The diocese has had to invest in a new vicarage; it has also had to find the resources to pay another priest.

This is reflected in the diocesan budget and in the share required of other parishes. Certainly, even with the new life injected, Lundwood cannot be self-sufficient. In other words, the cost of housing and stipend for the priest amount to more than the parish share paid by Lundwood. The balance is effectively provided by asking for more support from parishes which are stronger and generally exist in more privileged areas. Sometimes this puts very considerable demands upon other parish churches as they seek to raise their annual commitment to the diocese and the wider Church. If there is to be a real bias towards poorer areas, and if the Church is to remain committed to ministry in those areas, how can other parishes be persuaded to give sacrificially without it feeling like an unfair and crippling tax? It may be that some direct twinning of richer and poorer parishes, in a systematic way, is the way forward. In a direct and unmistakable way, this would emphasize the Church's continuing commitment to the poor. It may also help people within and beyond the formal boundaries of the Church, in both richer and poorer areas, to observe once again a much more direct relationship between religion and daily life. Such engagement will necessarily include the social impact of the gospel alongside worship. There are no flocks of sheep in Lundwood to provide the wherewithal for worship as there were in mediaeval Morebath. There will, however, be a conscious focus in Lundwood itself, and in any 'better-off' parish with which it might be twinned, on the inextricable links between the community's social needs and the worship of God in Jesus Christ. So now, pressing that point further still, how might faith be better manifested in the manner of our prayer, worship and contemplations?

Rediscovering the mystery

> What reason for that splendour of blue and gold
> For one so great and poor He was past all need?
> What but impetuous love that could not hold
> Its storm of spending and must scatter its seed
> In blue and gold and deed,
> And writes its busy Books on Books of Days
> To attempt and never touch the sum of praise.[28]

Edwin Muir, whose poetry we have been quoting, has behind him a fascinating story of faith. Brought up as an Orcadian, on those tough windswept islands to the north west of Scotland, whose version of the Christian faith was equally tough and windswept, he let go of the Christian faith as a young man. Sensitive and intelligent, he was sent as a late teenager to work in a Glasgow boneyard. Many of his siblings died in their youth from consumption. All this conspired to undermine his faith and to distance him from the tough Presbyterianism on which he had been nurtured. In his poem 'The Incarnate One', he vents his frustration at the harsh and prosaic pattern of worship and living he imbibed as a child:

> The Word made flesh here is made word again,
> A word made word in flourish and arrogant crook.
> See there King Calvin with his iron pen,
> And God three angry letters in a book . . .[29]

Muir married and moved on to work for the British Council, travelling widely across Europe. Later, despite the agnosticism of his equally sensitive and literary wife, Muir came back to faith. But the faith to which he returned was more nuanced, more sacramental, and led Muir back into the mystery, the narrative, which lies at the centre of the Christian message. Muir was now confronted with the greatness of this mystery and it was on this that he would feed for the rest of his life. A number of his later poems, including two on the Annunciation, are fashioned by this sacramental faith to which he returned. Indeed, the stanza with which we began sets the scene, with a vision to contemplate and then a conclusion leading from contemplation to praise. This call to worship is the third element, we would argue, that the Church needs to recover if it is to touch people's hearts.

There is, of course, one collection of experiences which, as we have already hinted, marks off the Church from every other caring agency. That set of experiences is contemplation, worship and prayer.[30] The key, then, is to offer this without any sense of apology and again with a true confidence in God, and alongside a real care for the poor. Here is another key opportunity to re-integrate the Christian narrative with the narrative of the world. One clear starting point is to re-introduce the Christian story, and indeed aspects of the 'cult', so to speak, back into people's lives. The wider Christian Church may learn here both from Roman Catholicism and from Orthodoxy. Both these traditions bring with them visual and dramatic pictures of the story. The crucifix, for long abhorred by Protestant Christians, is being rediscovered; in itself it tells the story. Icons, at one point in the early Middle Ages controversial even in Orthodoxy, set out the mystery graphically. Further, however, the drama of salvation is enacted in both the Roman Catholic and Orthodox traditions. Often people describe Orthodox liturgies as 'a little bit of heaven on earth'. These traditions cannot be seized or wrenched out of their context, but they can be sources for the rediscovery of the mystery across all Christian traditions. Even the re-introduction of these visual images, through crucifixes and icons, into people's domestic lives can begin to place the Christian narrative and mystery alongside people's daily experience. So often at baptisms, marriages and other points of religious encounter, the gifts offered are word-based – prayer books, Bibles, catechetical material. An icon or crucifix would speak far more eloquently, and particularly if the rite which accompanied it was vivid, dramatic and engaged the whole person.

Liturgical renewal which has happened effectively as an 'ecumenical phenomenon' assists in this process of rediscovering the mystery. Colour and drama are being re-appropriated by almost all traditions. Indeed, it was one of the Roman Catholic forerunners of liturgical renewal who most creatively explained this rediscovery of the mystery which can help form us both as individual Christians and as the Church of God. That forerunner was Dom Odo Casel, a Benedictine monk at the monastery of Maria Laach in the Rhineland. Sadly his works have not been translated into English and often his writing is obscure. He is most accessible through George Guiver's interpretation of him.[31] Encapsulating Casel's work in brief, Guiver writes:

> The gospel is about unique events through which the human situation has been changed. These events are not dead but alive. Basically, Casel says that Christian worship has a unique character which operates on the principle of the incarnation. It is sacramental. In it the events of Christ's life, death and rising become truly present.[32]

This, then, is the mystery with which we engage week by week, Sunday by Sunday, and in some cases weekday by weekday. Not only are these events saving events, they are sacramental. Guiver continues:

> Christian worship has the same sacramentality, and the role of Christ himself in all of it is sacramental. All of these things belong together as a whole; but they are also intimately related to 'secular' life as we live it, revealing its sacramental nature. This whole scheme is grounded in the New Testament, and its heart is the resurrection.[33]

This, then, impinges directly on the theme of this book. Through this understanding of worship, prayer and contemplation, the ordinary and the religious, the spiritual and the everyday are once again part of a seamless whole. There is, of course, a very sharp contrast between worship and the rest of daily life, but ultimately the two are welded together. There must be a sense of surprise within worship, but the experience of engaging with the mystery will transform the everyday. It is easy for the Church to become embarrassed by the incongruity or idiosyncratic nature of worship, as it is often seen by outsiders. Doubtless this is the reason why, in certain circles, robes and vestments are abandoned for lounge suits and sweaters. 'Café Church', too, tries to entice people into worship through the everyday experience of morning coffee or afternoon tea. Yet it is that 'experience of heaven on earth', seen in the Orthodox liturgy, which speaks more clearly of the mystery. Interestingly enough, evangelical Christianity has discovered colour, incense and other elements of worship, earlier seen as distinctive only of the Catholic tradition.

What precisely is the point of adopting a different vesture for worship? Certainly, it is not to re-invoke the Byzantine–Roman court from which chasubles and the like emerged. Rather, it is to help hold in tension the immanent and the transcendent in a Christian interpretation of our lives. We have made much already in this chapter of the importance of holding everyday life and religious experience together; God is immanent and available to us throughout the daily round. But God also calls us on. Jesus, in the words of the letter to the Hebrews, is our 'great high priest who ever lives to make intercession for us'. We are called by God to a perichoresis, a dance with the Deity himself. This is most perfectly offered for us in Jesus Christ. Different vesture, then, colour, drama and our sense of smell are imaginative aids to our appreciation of transcendence in God. Often we are far too tame in our use of drama and colour. We shall expand on this a little later.

So, this challenge or surprise is not a reversion to obscurity, or an escape into a recherché ecclesiastical world. Instead, Odo Casel sees the liturgy as a transformatory event. Each Sunday (or even weekday) the worshipper does not come for a refill of grace, rather like a car stopping at a filling station. Instead, the mystery of the Christian faith – that is the life, ministry, passion, death and resurrection of Jesus Christ – is enacted in the eucharistic liturgy, and thus made present for all. The *efficacy* of that mystery is also made present. People are taken down into that mystery and transformed by it. This transformation allows them, through both their presence and action, to live transformed lives which, in turn, can offer that same grace to transform others. They begin to live out what Paul describes as the 'new creation'.[34] The liturgical revival should make this easier to effect. In England, France and Germany, both Anglican and Roman Catholic religious communities have sometimes been able to offer this to the wider Christian Church.[35]

In the next five to ten years, the Church of England, through the work of its Liturgical Commission, intends to take this into the heart of people's lives. The past 30 years have seen the production of an entirely new generation of liturgical texts. The next phase of work is to help people use these in an imaginative pattern of formation. But, as we have hinted already, formation in worship is about formation in the Christian life. The liturgy is the unique place of encounter for *all* practising Christian people to begin to understand and live the mystery of the Christian story. What does this require, then, of us both in the Sunday liturgy and in the other key rites of passage? It means that the way in which the liturgy is celebrated is seminal to our living and learning as human beings. So music, silence, drama and vesture are crucial. This does not mean a seeking after gimmickry or a deliberate intention to shock. It means instead that the liturgy should be powerful in its ability to point to the transcendent God through whom we are magnetized to worship. Through this it can point forward to a transformation in the quality of our individual corporate lives.

The Sunday liturgy, then, is the equivalent of the food for our daily and weekly Christian journey. A remarkable treasure-house of material is now available, but it is still often not put to good use. There is room for far more silence in our weekly worship. At the end of the liturgy of the Word, and after communion there should be a marked silence to give an opportunity for real reflection upon the mystery which directs our lives. It is perhaps, the use of silence *corporately* of which we are still most frightened and which could do most to assist us in confronting and living the mystery which Casel commends. Music too remains in crisis. There has been something of a flight from traditional hymnody, with its ample doctrinal base, in favour of new and often trivial worship songs. There is, undoubtedly, some very good modern Christian music, but it is interesting that much of it is set within a comforting and even sentimental mood. Robust praise and even challenge in contemporary music are a necessary requirement.

Rites of passage, and especially baptism and confirmation, are another opportunity for a more radical shift in the setting of worship. The use of pilgrim liturgies within which the people move, and not only the ministers, can offer a much more vivid sense of journeying through the Christian life. The rediscovery of the Byzantine 'coffin-shaped' font, down into which we are taken with Christ into the grave to be raised with him as we emerge, is one welcome move. Cathedral confirmations have begun to rediscover that processional tradition for which great and lengthy gothic naves were originally constructed. Even allowing those who are baptized to be so soaked as to require a change of clothing offers imagery which speaks sharply of challenge and transformation. This parallels the more traditional challenge of the font placed as a deliberate impediment to progress inside the west door of a church. Movement from the font, to the centre of the church for confirmation, and then to the altar for the Eucharist, presses home the same transcendent message as do liturgical vestments, deliberately chosen for their 'setting worship apart' from other aspects of our life. Such pilgrimage liturgies, including baptisms and confirmations, require a drama and colour which speaks of the creative and redemptive power of God.

This regular encounter with the mystery of God and of God's story once again restores the unity of religion and everyday life which has been sundered over the centuries. It takes us back into the life of God. We shall be formed into the likeness of Christ; the Church can begin to live what St Paul describes as the 'new creation'.[36] This, then, together with a true confidence in God and a real care for the poor, may make possible that naturalness in religion and worship described in St George's Church in Tbilisi at the very beginning of this book. It is an experience and phenomenon beautifully described by Donald Nicholl in his book on the history of the Church in Russia over the past two centuries. Towards the end of that book, sometimes rather over-romantically, Nicholl picks up descriptions of natural religion within the Russian people. So, quoting Maurice Baring he notes: 'The Russian Church has the true smell: it smells of the poor, of untarred leather, onions and human sweat.'[37]

The entire chapter on the 'holy folk' captures this feeling more fully. Of course, the compromise and collaboration of the Russian Church with the former Soviet authorities needs to be held against this, but there remains a sense of the hearts of the poor still beating with the gospel, and certainly where piety has been preserved at its best. English culture is very different to the culture of either Russia or Georgia. Nevertheless, it is to a recapturing of religion touching the hearts of all people that this book looks forward. A renewed sense of confidence in God, of the rediscovery of the option for the poor and a lifelong engagement with the mystery are the starting point. That is all they are, and thereafter it is a matter of the grace of Our Lord Jesus Christ, the love of God and the fellowship of the Holy Spirit. For, ultimately, the entropy of the fragmented human spirit can only be reversed by the grace of God.

Notes

1 For Georgia, England and St George

1 Cf. John Finnis, *Natural Law and Natural Rights* (Oxford, Oxford University Press, 1979); Ian Ramsey, 'Towards a rehabilitation of natural law', in Ian Ramsey (ed.), *Christian Ethics and Contemporary Philosophy* (London, SCM Press, 1966), pp. 382–96; H. L. A. Hart, *The Concept of Law* (Oxford, Oxford University Press, 1961).
2 *The Poetical Works of Wordsworth*, ed. Paul D. Sheats (Boston, Houghton Mifflin, 1982), p. 353.
3 For background on St Kilda some of the best sources are: Tom Steel, *The Life and Death of St Kilda* (London, Fontana, 1978); David Quine, *St Kilda* (Grantown-on-Spey, Colin Baxter, 1995); Charles Maclean, *Island on the Edge of the World* (Edinburgh, Canongate, 1972); Meg Buchanan (ed.), *St Kilda: The Continuing Story of the Islands* (Edinburgh, HMSO, 1995).
4 D. H. Farmer (ed.) *The Age of Bede* (Harmondsworth, Penguin, 1965).
5 Adomnan of Iona, *Life of St Columba*, translated by Richard Sharpe (Harmondsworth, Penguin, 1995).
6 Fursey is referred to in the Venerable Bede, *The Ecclesiastical History of the English People* (Harmondsworth, Penguin, 1995), pp. 172–6.
7 For a fascinating account (part historical, part fiction) of the skelligs see Geoffrey Moorhouse, *Sun Dancing* (London, Weidenfeld and Nicolson, 1997).
8 Steel, *The Life and Death of St Kilda*, p. 110.
9 Edwin Muir, *Collected Poems* (London, Faber and Faber, 1960) p. 228.
10 Grace Davie, *Europe: The Exceptional Case* (London, Darton, Longman and Todd, 2002). See especially pp. 27–53.
11 Davie, *Europe*, p. 42.
12 Davie, *Europe*, p. 46.

2 Dismantling the scaffolding

1 *The Book of Margery Kempe*, translated by B. A. Windeatt (Harmondsworth, Penguin, 1985), Ch. 67, pp. 202 and 203.
2 Eamon Duffy, *The Voices of Morebath* (Cambridge, MA, Yale University Press, 2001).
3 Duffy, *Voices of Morebath*, p. 75.
4 Duffy, *Voices of Morebath*, p. 75.
5 Duffy, *Voices of Morebath*, pp. 27–8.

6 Christopher Haigh, *English Reformations* (Oxford, Oxford University Press, 1993). See also Diarmaid MacCulloch, *Tudor Church Militant* (Harmondsworth, Penguin, 1999).

7 Duffy, *Voices of Morebath*, p. 41.

8 In private conversation with the author.

9 Duffy, *Voices of Morebath*, p. 119.

10 See, again, MacCulloch, *Tudor Church Militant*; Haigh, *English Reformations*; and Diarmaid MacCulloch, *Thomas Cranmer, A Life* (Cambridge, MA, Yale University Press, 1996).

3 Hearts strangely cooled?

1 Quoted in Roger Lloyd, *The Church of England, 1900–1965* (London, SCM Press, 1966), p. 195.

2 Edwin Markham, 'Outwitted', in *The Poems of Edwin Markham*, ed. C. L. Wallis (London, Harper, 1959).

3 Diarmaid MacCulloch, *Reformation: Europe's House Divided 1490–1700* (London, Allen Lane, 2003) p. 392.

4 See Trevor Beeson, *The Deans* (London, SCM Press, 2004), Ch. 10, 'The parish priest: William Butler, Lincoln', p. 90.

5 Quoted in Stephen Platten (ed.), *Anglicanism and the Western Christian Tradition* (Norwich, Canterbury Press, 2003), p. 122.

6 See, for example, Holy Trinity parish church at Berwick-upon-Tweed.

7 MacCulloch, *Reformation*, p. 526.

8 MacCulloch, *Reformation*, p. 528.

9 Diarmaid MacCulloch reflects on this vividly in his review of Patrick Collinson's *From Cranmer to Sancroft* (London, Continuum, 2006) in *The Spectator*, 23 September 2006.

10 Christopher Dawson, *Understanding Europe* (London, Sheed and Ward, 1952) p. 35. For a more detailed study of the cultural and religious effects of the Reformation and its aftermath see Christopher Dawson, *The Dividing of Christendom* (London, Sidgwick and Jackson, 1971).

11 Cf. Doreen Rosman, *The Evolution of the English Churches 1500–2000* (Cambridge, Cambridge University Press, 2003), pp. 147–8.

12 See Henry Rack, *Reasonable Enthusiast: John Wesley and the Rise of Methodism* (third edition, London, Epworth Press, 2002), p. 360.

13 Rupert Davies, *Methodism* (Harmondsworth, Pelican, 1963), p. 125.

14 Rack, *Reasonable Enthusiast*, pp. 296ff.

15 W. M. Jacob, *Lay People and Religion in the Early Eighteenth Century* (Cambridge, Cambridge University Press, 1996), p. 16.

16 Jacob, *Lay People*, p. 17; cf. also p. 123.

17 Jacob, *Lay People*, p. 174.

18 Jacob, *Lay People*, p. 228.

19 Jacob, *Lay People*, p. 228.

20 Cf. Flora Thompson, *Lark Rise to Candleford* (Oxford, Oxford University Press, 1945), p. 205.
21 Rack, *Reasonable Enthusiast*, p. 313.

4 Revivals and refusals

1 Robin Gill, *The Myth of the Empty Church* (London, SPCK, 1993).
2 Philip Snowden, *An Autobiography* (London, Ivor Nicholson and Watson, 1934), Vol. I, pp. 101–2.
3 Snowden, *Autobiography*, Vol. I, p. 63.
4 Peter Berger, Brigitte Berger and Hansfried Kellner, *The Homeless Mind* (Harmondsworth, Penguin, 1974), p. 140.
5 Owen Chadwick, *The Secularisation of the European Mind in the Nineteenth Century* (Cambridge, Cambridge University Press, 1975), p. 94.
6 Anthony Symondson (ed.), *The Victorian Crisis of Faith* (London, SPCK, 1970).
7 Chadwick, *Secularisation*, p. 6.
8 Edmund Gosse, *Father and Son* (London, William Heinemann, 1907).
9 Gosse, quoted in Evan Charteris, *The Life and Letters of Sir Edmund Gosse* (London, Heinemann, 1931), p. 505.
10 Gosse, *Father and Son*, p. 111.
11 Ann Thwaite, *Glimpses of the Wonderful: The Life of Philip Henry Gosse* (London, Faber & Faber, 2002).
12 Charles Dickens, *Bleak House* (Harmondsworth, Penguin, 1994), pp. 595–6.
13 This point is made more generally about modernity by Peter Berger *et al.*, *Homeless Mind*, Introduction, pp. 11–25; and also Chapter 3, pp. 62–77; Chapter 6, pp. 126–42; Chapter 8, pp. 163–79. See also Chadwick, *Secularisation*.
14 A. N. Wilson, *The Victorians* (London, Hutchinson, 2002), p. 433.
15 Cf. Stephen Platten, 'Thomas Hardy's flawed universe', *Modern Churchman*, Vol. XXVIII, No. 1 (1985), pp. 17–26.
16 Thomas Hardy, *Collected Poems* (London, Macmillan, 1976), p. 561.
17 Hardy, *Collected Poems*, p. 562.
18 Flora Thompson, *Lark Rise to Candleford* (Oxford, Oxford University Press, 1945), p. 205.
19 John Henry Newman, *An Essay on the Development of Christian Doctrine* (Harmondsworth, Penguin, 1974).
20 Cf., here, Owen Chadwick, *From Bossuet to Newman* (Cambridge, Cambridge University Press, 1957).
21 This argument is explored in Stephen Platten and George Pattison, *Spirit and Tradition: An Essay on Change* (Norwich, Canterbury Press, 1996), especially Chapters 1–3, pp. 5–63.

22 Cf. notes 15 and 16 above.

23 Charles F. Lowder, *Twenty-one Years in St George's Mission* (London, Rivingtons, 1877), p. 37.

24 See Graham Davies, 'Squires in the East End?' *Theology*, Vol. LXXXVI, No. 712 (July 1983), pp. 249–59.

25 Wilson, *The Victorians*, pp. 541–2.

5 Never such innocence again

1 Philip Larkin, 'MCMXIV', in Philip Larkin, *Collected Poems* (London, Faber & Faber, London, 1988), p. 127.

2 Eric Hobsbawm, *Age of Extremes: The Short Twentieth Century. 1914–1991* (London, Michael Joseph, 1994).

3 John Henry Newman, *An Essay on the Development of Christian Doctrine* (1845 edition, Harmondsworth, Penguin, 1973).

4 George Tyrrell, *Christianity at the Cross-Roads* (London, Longmans, Green, 1910), pp. 41–2.

5 Tyrrell, *Cross-Roads*, p. 44.

6 *Through Scylla and Charibdis; Or, The Old Theology and the New* (London, Longmans, Green, 1907), p. 374.

7 Tyrrell, *Cross-Roads*, p. 275.

8 A. R. Vidler, *A Variety of Catholic Modernists* (Cambridge, Cambridge University Press, 1970), p. 16.

9 A. R. Vidler, *Twentieth Century Defenders of the Faith* (London, SCM Press, 1965), p. 46.

10 Gabriel Daly OSA, *Transcendence and Immanence* (Oxford, Clarendon Press, 1980), p. 1, quoting Ludwig Ott.

11 Daly, *Transcendence*, p. 3.

12 Daly, *Transcendence*, p. 231.

13 Daly, *Transcendence*, p. 199.

14 Thomas Hardy, *Collected Poems* (London, Macmillan, 1976), p. 542.

15 Rudyard Kipling, 'Common Form', in *Rudyard Kipling's Verse, Definitive Edition* (London, Hodder & Stoughton, 1940), p. 390.

16 Rudyard Kipling, 'Gethsemane', in *Rudyard Kipling's Verse*, p. 98.

17 Thomas Hardy, 'Men Who March Away', in *Collected Poems*, p. 493.

18 Paul Fussell, *The Great War and Modern Memory* (Oxford, Oxford University Press, 1975), p. 21.

19 Wilfred Owen, 'Parable of the Old Man and the Young', in *The Collected Poems of Wilfred Owen*, ed. C. Day-Lewis (London, Chatto and Windus, 1963), p. 42.

20 Alan Wilkinson, *The Church of England and the First World War* (London, SPCK, 1978).

21 Wilkinson, *Church of England*, p. 244.

22 Geoffrey Studdert-Kennedy, 'High and Lifted Up', in Geoffrey Studdert-Kennedy, *The Unutterable Beauty* (London, Hodder & Stoughton, 1927).

23 R. E. Roberts, *H. R. L. Sheppard, His Life and Letters* (London, John Murray, 1942), pp. 91–2.

24 Alan Wilkinson, *Dissent or Conform: War, Peace and the English Churches 1900–1945* (London, SCM Press, 1986), p. 114.

25 W. H. Auden, 'Refugee Blues', in W. H. Auden, *Collected Shorter Poems 1927–1957* (London, Faber & Faber, 2003).

26 Sidney Keyes, 'War Poet', in Sidney Keyes, *Collected Poems* (Manchester: Carcanet, 2002).

27 Herbert Read, 'To a Conscript of 1940', in Hugh Haughton (ed.) *Second World War Poems* (London, Faber & Faber, 2004), p. 228.

28 Cf. his influential bestseller: William Temple, *Christianity and the Social Order* (London, SCM Press, 1942).

29 Peter Hennessy, *Never Again: Britain 1945–1951* (London, Jonathan Cape, 1992), p. 22.

30 Hennessy, *Never Again*, p. 436.

31 Cf., here, Matthew Grimley, *Citizenship, Community and the Church of England: Liberal Anglican Theories of the State between the Wars* (Oxford Historical Monographs, Oxford, Oxford University Press, 2004). See especially p. 225, his note of the Anglicanism of Temple and others 'providing a theoretical underpinning for English civil religion. It offered a providentialist account of national history and destiny.'

32 J. A. T. Robinson, *Honest to God* (London, SCM Press, 1963).

33 For a brief survey of this period cf. Stephen Platten, 'Thirty years on', *New Fire*, Vol. VI, No. 46 (Spring 1981), pp. 274–80. See also T. J. Altizer and W. Hamilton, *Radical Theology and the Death of God* (Harmondsworth, Penguin, 1968); Paul van Buren, *The Secular Meaning of the Gospel* (London, SCM Press, 1966); Harvey Cox, *The Secular City* (London, SCM Press, 1966).

34 Alan Richardson and John Bowden (eds), *A New Dictionary of Christian Theology* (London, SCM Press, 1983), p. 146; E. A. Livingstone and F. L. Cross (eds) *The Oxford Dictionary of the Christian Church* (third edition, Oxford, Oxford University Press, 1997), p. 459.

35 See, for example. Grace Davie, *Europe: The Exceptional Case* (London, Darton, Longman and Todd, 2002); Grace Davie, *Religion in Europe: A Memory Mutates* (Oxford, Oxford University Press, 2000). See also the recent writings of David Martin and the expansive literature on the rise of Islam.

36 See E. R. Wickham, *Church and People in an Industrial City* (London, Lutterworth Press, 1957).

37 Douglas Rhymes, *Prayer in the Secular City* (London, Lutterworth Press, 1967).

38 John Hick, *God and the Universe of Faiths* (London, Macmillan, 1973).

39 Two of the key volumes here are: Alan Race, *Interfaith Encounter* (London, SCM Press, 2001) and Paul Knitter, *No Other Name?* (London, Orbis Books, 1985).

6 And into a brave new world?

1 David Lodge, *How Far Can You Go?* (Harmondsworth, Penguin, 1981), p. 169.

2 See Stephen Platten, 'The conflict over the control of elementary education 1870–1902 and its effect upon the life and influence of the Church', *British Journal of Education Studies*, Vol. XXII, No. 3 (October 1978).

3 This is set out in journalistic summary form by A. N. Wilson in his *After the Victorians* (London, Hutchinson, 2005), pp. 509–12. For a more considered account see Peter Hennessy, *Never Again* (London, Jonathan Cape, 1992), especially Chapter 4.

4 Cf. Stephen Platten (ed.), *The Retreat of the State* (Norwich, Canterbury Press, 1999).

5 *The Way Ahead: Church of England Schools in the New Millennium* (GS1406) (London, Church House Publishing, 2001), otherwise known as the Dearing Report.

6 Bryan R. Wilson, 'Secularisation', in Paul Barry Clarke and Andrew Linzey (eds) *Dictionary of Ethics, Theology and Society* (London, Routledge, 1996), p. 747.

7 Owen Chadwick, *The Secularisation of the European Mind in the Nineteenth Century* (Cambridge, Cambridge University Press, 1975), p. 258.

8 Grace Davie, *Religion in Modern Europe: A Memory Mutates* (Oxford, Oxford University Press, 2000), p. 1.

9 Steve Bruce, *From Cathedrals to Cults: Religion in the Modern World* (Oxford, Oxford University Press, 1996), p. 230, quoted in Grace Davie, *Europe: The Exceptional Case* (London, Darton, Longman and Todd, 2002), p. 14. See also Davie, *Religion*, p. 26.

10 Callum G. Brown, *The Death of Christian Britain* (London, Routledge, 2001), p. 1.

11 Brown, *Death of Christian Britain*, p. 2.

12 Davie, *Europe*, p. 21.

13 Here, cf. David Martin, *On Secularisation: Towards a Revised General Theory* (Aldershot, Ashgate, 2005). The shifts are particularly clearly catalogued on pp. 140–54, where he analyses the rise of modern Pentecostalism.

14 Davie, *Religion*, p. 26.

15 Martin, *On Secularisation*, p. 3.

16 Harvey Cox, *The Secular City* (London, SCM Press, 1965), pp. 20–1.

17 Cox, *Secular City*, pp. 69–70.

18 Cox, *Secular City*, p. 260.
19 Cox, *Secular City*, p. 265.
20 Douglas Rhymes, *Prayer in the Secular City* (London, Lutterworth Press, 1967).
21 J. A. T. Robinson, *Honest to God* (London, SCM Press, 1963).
22 J. A. T. Robinson, 'The debate continues', in J. A. T. Robinson and David Edwards, *The Honest to God Debate* (London, SCM Press, 1963), p. 249.
23 Robinson, 'The debate continues', p. 275.
24 Rudolph Bultmann, *A History of the Synoptic Tradition*, English translation John Marsh (Oxford, Basil Blackwell, 1963).
25 Rudolph Bultmann, *The Gospel of John*, English translation G. R. Beasley-Murray (Oxford, Basil Blackwell, 1971).
26 Here, see H. Bartsch (ed.), *Kerygma and Myth*, English translation R. Fuller. London, SPCK, 1964); Rudolph Bultmann, *Jesus Christ and Mythology* (New York, Charles Scribners' Sons, 1958); Rudolph Bultmann, *Theology of the New Testament. Vols. I & II* (London, SCM Press, 1952, 1955).
27 Cf., here, Peter Brown, *The Cult of the Saints* (London, SCM Press, 1981); Jonathan Sumption, *Pilgrimage* (London, Faber & Faber, 1975, 2002), especially Chapters II, III, IV and V; and also Keith Thomas, *Religion and the Decline of Magic* (new edited edition, Harmondsworth, Penguin, 1991).
28 Cf. Paul Tillich, *The Shaking of the Foundations* (Harmondsworth, Penguin, 1962).
29 See Paul Tillich, *The Courage to Be* (London, Fontana, 1962).
30 Paul Tillich, *Systematic Theology* (Welwyn Garden City, James Nisbet, 1968).
31 Cf. Stephen Platten, 'Europe come of age', *Theology*, Vol. XCVIII, No. 782 (March–April 1995), pp. 100–10. And for a recent example, Stanley Hauerwas, 'Making the Church visible: the Sermon on the Mount. Lessons learned from Bonhoeffer and Yoder', *Crucible* (October–December 2006).
32 Dietrich Bonhoeffer, *Letters and Papers from Prison* (London, SCM Press, 1971).
33 Eberhard Bethge, *Dietrich Bonhoeffer* (München, Kaiser, 1967), p. 831.
34 Dietrich Bonhoeffer, *Ethics* (London, SCM Press, 1978).
35 Colin Slee (ed.) *Honest to God: Forty Years On* (London, SCM Press, 2004), p. 21.
36 Chadwick, *Secularisation*, p. 264.
37 Bonhoeffer, *Ethics*, p. 346.
38 Chadwick, *Secularisation*, p. 263.
39 John de Gruchy, *Being Human* (London, SCM Press, 2006), p. 104, makes this point powerfully, also embracing Bonhoeffer.

40 W. H. Auden, *Collected Poems* (London, Faber & Faber, 1976), pp. 509–10.

7 Circling them in or out?

1 'Outwitted', in *The Poems of Edwin Markham*, ed. C. L. Wallis (London, Harper, 1959).

2 John A. T. Robinson, *On Being the Church in the World* (Harmondsworth, Penguin, 1969), p. 7.

3 Robinson, *On Being the Church*, p. 38.

4 H. Benedict Green, *The Gospel According to St Matthew* (Oxford, Oxford University Press, 1975), p. 127.

5 David Hill, *The Gospel of Matthew* (London, Oliphants, 1972), p. 217.

6 D. E. Nineham, *The Gospel of St Mark* (London, A. & C. Black, 1963), p. 253.

7 Cf. E. P. Sanders, *Jesus and Judaism* (London, SCM Press, 1985) and *Paul and Palestinian Judaism* (London, SCM Press, 1985).

8 Cf. Martin Hengel, *Judaism and Hellenism* (two volumes, London, SCM Press, 1974).

9 Ernst Käsemann, *The Testament of Jesus* (London, SCM Press, 1968), pp. 75–6.

10 Oscar Cullmann, *The Johannine Circle* (London, SCM Press, 1975), p. 35.

11 Günther Bornkamm, *Paul* (London, Hodder & Stoughton, 1971), p. 162.

12 R. M. Grant, *Gnosticism and Early Christianity* (Oxford, Oxford University Press, 1959), p. 182.

13 Grant, *Gnosticism*, p. 185.

14 Robert. L. Wilken, *The Myth of Christian Beginnings* (London, SCM Press, 1971), p. 50.

15 Wilken, *Myth of Christian Beginnings*, p. 158.

16 Wilken, *Myth of Christian Beginnings*, p. 206 but quoting Gregory of Nyssa, *Commentaries in Canticum Canticorum* (5:2), Bratis XI.

17 Wilken, *Myth of Christian Beginnings*, p. 206.

18 The Venerable Bede, *The Ecclesiastical History of the English People* (revised edition, Harmondsworth, Penguin, 1990), p. 92.

19 H. Richard Niebuhr, *Christ and Culture* (London, Faber & Faber, 1952), p. 18.

20 T. J. Gorringe, *Furthering Humanity* (Aldershot, Ashgate, 2004), pp. 12–16, criticizes Niebuhr's typology, notably for its tendency to elide the anthropological notion of culture with that of 'high culture'. Gorringe's own critique, however, is too dismissive of Niebuhr's approach. There is no doubt that the term 'culture' is a slippery concept, as Gorringe argues. Even so, Niebuhr's contrasting categories still offer an initial and broad distinction between

the way in which different groups either respond to or reject the Christian tradition.

21 Niebuhr, *Christ and Culture*, p. 253.

22 Cf., here, John Milbank, *Theology and Social Theory* (Oxford, Basil Blackwell, 1990).

23 For a brief but fuller description of Radical Orthodoxy see my article, 'Jesus and Radical Orthodoxy', in J. L. Houlden (ed.), *Jesus in History, Thought and Culture: An Encyclopaedia* (two volumes, Santa Barbara and Oxford, ABC Clio, 2003), pp. 715–17.

24 Cf. his Gifford Lectures: Stanley Hauerwas, *With the Grain of the Universe* (London, SCM Press, 2002), especially Chapter 4. Earlier on he establishes the primacy of virtue and character in Stanley Hauerwas, *Character and the Christian Life* (San Antonio, Trinity University Press, 1975) and *The Peaceable Kingdom* (London, SCM Press, 1983). See also Samuel Wells' constructive criticism of Hauerwas and his criticisms of Niebuhr in *Transforming Fate into Destiny* (Carlisle, Paternoster, 1998).

25 See here particularly Reinhold Niebuhr, *Leaves from the Notebook of a Tamed Cynic* (San Francisco, Harper & Row, 1980) and Reinhold Niebuhr, *Moral Man and Immoral Society* (New York, Charles Scribners' Sons, 1932).

26 Stanley Hauerwas, *Wilderness Wanderings: Probing Twentieth Century Theology and Philosophy* (Oxford, Westview Press, 1997), p. 1.

27 Hauerwas, *Wilderness Wanderings*, p. 157.

28 Fergus Kerr OP, *Immortal Longings: Versions of Transcending Humanity* (London, SPCK, 1997), p. vii.

29 Kerr, *Immortal Longings*, p. 85.

30 H. Richard Niebuhr, *Christ and Culture*, p. 247.

31 Reinhold Niebuhr, *The Children of Light and the Children of Darkness* (London, Nisbet, 1945), p. vi.

32 Attributed to Reinhold from Richard Fox, *Reinhold Niebuhr: A Biography* (New York, Pantheon Books, 1985), p. 290.

33 Cf. Reinhold Niebuhr, *Moral Man and Immoral Society* (New York, Charles Scribners' Sons, 1932). See also his *Leaves from the Notebook of a Tamed Cynic*.

34 Markham, 'Outwitted'.

8 Herding cats?

1 T.S. Eliot, 'Macavity: the Mystery Cat', from *Old Possum's Book of Practical Cats* in *The Complete Poems and Plays* (London, Faber & Faber, 1942), pp. 226–7.

2 Eliot, 'The Ad-dressing of Cats', *Old Possum*, pp. 234–5.

3 *New Statesman*, 25 February 2002.

4 Tim Gorringe in *Furthering Humanity* (Aldershot, Ashgate, 2004). These two movements paradoxically continue alongside each other.

5 For an excellent analysis of this haphazard process into the age of Constantine see Robin Lane Fox, *Pagans and Christians* (Harmondsworth, Viking, 1986). For larger panoramas still, see Richard Fletcher, *The Conversion of Europe: From Paganism to Christianity. 371–1386* (London, HarperCollins, 1987); Peter Brown, *The Rise of Western Christendom* (Oxford, Basil Blackwell, 1996); Judith Herrin, *The Formation of Christendom* (Oxford, Basil Blackwell, 1987).

6 Augustine, *The City of God*, translated by Henry Bettenson (Harmondsworth, Pelican, 1972).

7 Diarmaid MacCulloch, *Reformation: Europe's House Divided 1490–1700* (London, Allen Lane, 2003), p. 35.

8 MacCulloch, *Reformation*, p. 53.

9 Christopher Dawson, *Understanding Europe* (London, Sheed and Ward, 1952), pp. 31ff.

10 Christopher Dawson, *The Dividing of Christendom* (London, Sheed and Ward, 1965), p. 13.

11 Dawson, *Christendom*, pp. 13 and 14.

12 Dawson, *Christendom*, pp. 19–22.

13 Alexander Pope, *An Essay on Man* (1733), Part 2, 1.1.

14 Iris Murdoch, *Metaphysics as a Guide to Morals* (London, Chatto and Windus, 1992), pp. 511–12.

15 Alasdair MacIntyre, *After Virtue* (London, Duckworth, 1981), p. 35.

16 MacIntyre, *After Virtue*, p. 38.

17 MacIntyre, *After Virtue*, pp. 154ff.

18 MacIntyre, *After Virtue*, p. 50.

19 MacIntyre, *After Virtue*, p. 241.

20 This is described most vividly in Simon Schama's excellent narrative history of the French Revolution; Simon Schama, *Citizens: A Chronicle of the French Revolution* (Harmondsworth, Penguin, 2004).

21 Conor Cruise O'Brien, *The Great Melody: A Thematic Biography of Edmund Burke* (London, Sinclair Stevenson, 1992).

22 Quoted in O'Brien, *Great Melody*, p. 452.

23 O'Brien, *Great Melody*, p. 453. See also Edmund Burke, *Reflections on the Revolution in France* (Harmondsworth, Penguin, 1986).

24 Louis MacNeice, 'Snow' (second stanza), in Louis MacNeice, *Collected Poems* (London, Faber & Faber, 1966), p. 30.

25 George Steiner, *After Babel: Aspects of Language and Translation* (New York and London, Oxford University Press, 1975), p. 474.

26 George Steiner, *Real Presences* (London, Faber & Faber, 1989), p. 3.

27 MacIntyre, *After Virtue*, p. 245.

9 Between two worlds or more?

1 Matthew Arnold, 'Stanzas from the Grande Chartreuse', in *The Works of Matthew Arnold* (Ware, Wordsworth, 1995), p. 272.

2 Arnold, *Works*, p. 402.
3 Thomas Hardy, *Tess of the D'Urbervilles* (London, Macmillan, 1962), pp. 414–15.
4 Hardy, *Tess*, p. 470.
5 Thomas Hardy, 'The Oxen', in Thomas Hardy, *Collected Poems* (London, Macmillan, 1976), p. 468.
6 Hardy, 'The Darkling Thrush', in *Collected Poems*, p. 150.
7 Philip Jenkins, *The Next Christendom: The Coming of Global Christianity* (Oxford, Oxford University Press, 2002).
8 See, for example, Timothy Yates (ed.), *Mission and the Next Christendom* (Calver, Cliff College Publishing, 2005).
9 Darrell Jackson, 'Pax Europa: Crux Europe' in Yates, *Mission*, pp. 85–106.
10 There is, of course, the exception of fundamentalist groups in the southern states of the USA and some conservative Pentecostalist groups peppered across North America and Western Europe.
11 Hardy, *Collected Poems*, p. 306.
12 Hardy, *Collected Poems*, p. 113.
13 Owen Chadwick, *The Secularisation of the European Mind in the Nineteenth Century* (Cambridge, Cambridge University Press, 1975).
14 See Diarmaid MacCulloch, *Tudor Church Militant: Edward VI and the Protestant Reformation* (Harmondsworth, Penguin, 1999).
15 See Pauline Croft, 'The new English Church in one family: William, Mildred and Robert Cecil,' in Stephen Platten (ed.), *Anglicanism and the Western Christian Tradition* (Norwich, Canterbury Press, 2003), pp. 65–89.
16 Paul Fussell, *The Great War and Modern Memory* (Oxford, Oxford University Press, 1975), pp. 3, 6.
17 Cf. Jürgen Moltmann, *The Crucified God* (London, SCM Press, 1974); but more particularly on Geoffrey Studdert-Kennedy, see Jürgen Moltmann, *The Trinity and the Kingdom of God* (London, SCM Press, 1981), pp. 347, 228.
18 Viigo Mortensen, 'Global Christianity is changing. How do these changes influence conflict and peace?' in Yates, *Mission*, p. 53.
19 Mortensen, 'Global Christianity', p. 51.
20 Mortensen, 'Global Christianity', p. 52.
21 W. M. Jacob, *Lay People and Religion in the Early Eighteenth Century* (Cambridge, Cambridge University Press, 1996).

10 Reversing entropy

1 Edwin Muir, 'The Church', in Edwin Muir, *Collected Poems* (London, Faber & Faber, 1960), p. 263.
2 Even the writers and researchers for *Mission-Shaped Church* (London, Church House Publishing, 2004) fell into this trap. Their desire here was to identify modern culture and to angle the

Christian message, using the techniques which modern culture itself manifests and uses.

3 Peter Berger, *A Rumour of Angels* (Harmondsworth: Penguin, 1969).

4 Claire Tomalin, *Thomas Hardy: The Time-Torn Man* (Harmondsworth, Penguin, 2006).

5 See, again, Stephen Platten, 'Thomas Hardy's flawed universe', *Modern Churchman*, New Series, Vol. XXVII, No. 1 (1985), pp. 17–26.

6 Muir, *Collected Poems*, pp. 263–4.

7 Edwin Muir, 'The Incarnate One', in *Collected Poems*, p. 228.

8 Berger, *Rumour of Angels*, Chapter 1, pp. 13ff.

9 J. Andrew Kirk, *Mission Under Scrutiny* (London, Darton, Longman and Todd, 2006), pp. 206–7.

10 Kirk, *Mission*, p. 65.

11 Here, cf. Austin Farrer, *The Glass of Vision* (London, Dacre Press, 1948).

12 Berger, *Rumour of Angels*, p. 72.

13 Anthony Russell, *The Country Parish* (London, SPCK, 1986), p. 63.

14 Russell, *Country Parish*, p. 103.

15 Christopher C. Knight, 'Unjust war? The September attacks and the attack on modernity', *Theology*, Vol. CV, No. 826 (July–August 2002), p. 260.

16 Knight, 'Unjust war?', p. 262.

17 Angela Tilby, *Won't You Join the Dance* (London, SPCK, 1985) and *Science and the Soul* (London, SPCK, 1992). See also the journalistic work of Bishop Richard Harries on the radio and in newspapers; some of his published writings are also apologetic in nature.

18 Muir, *Collected Poems*, p. 263.

19 Muir, *Collected Poems*, p. 264.

20 Tim Gorringe (*Furthering Humanity*, Aldershot, Ashgate, 2004) makes this point forcibly in a number of places; cf. especially pp. 129ff. and Ch. 7.

21 Luke 10.3.

22 Luke 12.33.

23 David Sheppard, *Bias to the Poor* (London, Hodder & Stoughton, 1973).

24 *Faith in the City* (London, Church House Publishing, 1984).

25 Alan Wilkinson, *The Church of England and the First World War* (London, SPCK, 1978).

26 R. S. Thomas, *Later Poems* (London, Macmillan, 1983), p. 35.

27 This was televised as the three programmes in the Channel Four *Priest Idol* series.

28 Muir, *Collected Poems*, p. 263.

29 Muir, *Collected Poems*, p. 228.

30 This point has been argued both beautifully and persuasively by Samuel Wells in his *God's Companions: Re-imaging Christian Ethics* (Oxford, Basil Blackwell, 2006).

31 George Guiver CR, *Pursuing the Mystery* (London, SPCK, 1996).

32 Guiver, *Pursuing the Mystery*, p. 56.

33 Guiver, *Pursuing the Mystery*, p. 57.

34 Cf. 2 Cor. 5.17: 'Therefore, if anyone is in Christ, he is a new creation; the old has passed away, behold the new has come.'

35 So, for example, at En Calcut, near Castres in south-west France; at Casel's own monastery, Maria Laach, near Koblenz, in the Rhineland; and at the Anglican women's community at Tŷ Mawr in south-east Wales (cf. Philip Toynbee, *Part of a Journey: An Autobiographical Journal 1977–1979*, London, Collins, 1981).

36 2 Cor. 5.17.

37 Donald Nicholl, *Triumphs of the Spirit in Russia* (London, Darton, Longman and Todd, 1997), p. 211.

Index

Index